1965

The Christmas Book

Celebrating Christmas in All Nations

Gadshill Place
Home of Charles Dickens

"I have always thought of Christmas as a good time; a kind, forgiving, charitable, pleasant time; the only time I know of in the long calendar of the year when men and women seem, by one consent, to open their shut-up hearts freely."

Charles Dickens

The Christmas Book

edited by

Marion R. Todd

THE WILLIAM-FREDERICK PRESS

391 EAST 149TH STREET   NEW YORK 55, N.Y.

My mother and my husband and my son,
Grandchildren, godchildren of various ages—
To those who saw my Christmas book begun
I dedicate with love the finished pages.

Written especially for Marion R. Todd
and presented to her in the spirit
of Christmas giving
by Robert Hillyer

In This Collection ...

Foreword

by Nora Waln

CHRISTMAS is always a happy time, when families unite in celebration, when the sins of the world are temporarily forgotten, when "Peace on Earth, Good will to Men" prevail universally.

It is a joy to be associated with the *Christmas Book*, which I know will bring great pleasure and happiness to all.

Christmas is one of the biggest days in the life of Marion Todd (her family founded Greenwich, Connecticut, in 1640). On this day her family, godchildren and friends gather at her home for an old New England Christmas. It is therefore appropriate that the day be marked with a book which will find an honored niche in many homes, its significance increasing with each passing year, a book which will, it seems safe to predict, be brought out as the season approaches with the lights, the decorations, the tinsel and carol books, to play its part in the holiday proceedings.

I quote here Henry Wadsworth Longfellow's

> *I heard the bells on Christmas Day*
> *Their old familiar carols play*
> *And wild and sweet, the words repeat,*
> *"Peace on Earth, Good will to Men."*

"Dobin's"
Fulmer, Buckinghamshire
England

The Birth of Jesus

Luke 2: 8-20

AND there were in the same country shepherds abiding in the field, keeping watch over their flock by night. And an angel of the Lord stood by them, and the glory of the Lord shone round about them: and they were sore afraid. And the angel said unto them, Be not afraid; for, behold, I bring you good tidings of great joy which shall be to all people. For there is born to you this day in the city of David a Saviour, who is Christ the Lord. And this is the sign unto you: Ye shall find a babe wrapped in swaddling clothes, lying in a manger. And suddenly there was with the angel a multitude of the heavenly host praising God, and saying,

> Glory to God in the highest,
> And on earth peace among men
> In whom He is well pleased.

And it came to pass, when the angels went away from them into heaven, the shepherds said one to another, Let us now go even unto Bethlehem, and see this thing that is come to pass, which the Lord hath made known unto us. And they came with haste, and found both Mary and Joseph, and the babe lying in the manger.

And when they saw it, they made known concerning the saying which was spoken to them about this child. And all that heard it wondered at the things which were spoken unto them by the shepherds.

But Mary kept all these sayings, pondering them in her heart. And the shepherds returned, glorifying and praising God for all the things that they had heard and seen, even as it was spoken unto them.

Christmas in Many Lands

Christmas in North America

by Marion R. Todd

THE Christ Child's birthday, our most religious holiday, is celebrated both by Catholics and Protestants in North America. It is also a time when families gather and exchange gifts, and children watch for the arrival of Santa Claus or St. Nick, as the venerable "old man from the North" is sometimes called.

The first Christmas in North America was celebrated in the South at Jamestown Colony in Virginia in 1619. (Though Jamestown was settled in 1607, Christmas was not celebrated until the womenfolk arrived years later.) According to Captain John Smith's *Journal*, "The extreme winde, rayne, frost and snow caused us to keep Christmas among the savages where we were never more merry, nor fed on more plenty of good Oysters, Fish, Flesh, Wild Fowl and goode Bread, nor never had better fires in England."

Down through the years the Virginians were noted for their lavish yuletide hospitality. The plantation owners entertained for weeks at a time. The great houses were beautifully decorated with greens, the rooms brilliantly illuminated with many candles, romantic mistletoe in each room. There was dancing and singing in the master's house and in the Negro cabins. The tremendous fireplace burned hickory logs, and in the large kitchen, usually in a separate building, the colored cook and her extra helpers brought in for this occasion worked from morn till night preparing their delicious food specialities and trying to outdo the "Aunties" on the neighboring plantations.

Religious ceremonies were held in churches decorated with greens. It was a time of peace, plenty and merriment — the most joyous and festive of all holidays!

In the early Dutch settlement at Niew Amsterdam on Manhattan Island (now New York) the first church was named in honor of St. Nicholas, the patron saint of the new colony. The good Dutch families loved Christmas with its joyful times amid much merriment. The sturdy old city fathers decreed that all official offices be closed on December 14, not to be reopened until three weeks after Christmas. The Dutch churches and homes were decorated with evergreens and all the families planned large feasts. Trees for the children were laden with gifts. On Twelfth-Night, the twelfth day after Christmas, the Christmas trees were taken down and burned.

The first Christmas in New England, in 1620, was not celebrated by the Pilgrims of the Plymouth Colony of Massachusetts. Governor William Bradford stated in his *Journal:* "And ye 25 day [of December] begane [the

Pilgrims] to erecte ye first house for comone use to receive them and their goods." Governor Bradford does not mention the day as Christmas, for these early settlers did not celebrate the day; instead, the first home-making of our New England ancestors was started on Christmas Day. However, in 1686 Governor Andros held Christmas service in Town House; this is believed to be the first legal observance of Christmas in Boston. Since then, Boston and its environs have ranked among the great Christmas centers of the North American continent. In 1856 Governor Nathaniel P. Banks made December 25 a legal holiday in Massachusetts.

Boston is noted for its beautiful yuletide ceremonies and carol singing on Beacon Hill. Many New England towns display elaborate crèches portraying the Nativity, some with live animals and human attendants.

This beautiful custom of crèches is becoming nationwide. How wonderful to attend a Christmas Eve midnight service or mass and then leave the church and see a "live" Nativity.

Christmas derives its name from "Christ Mass," or the service honoring the birth of Jesus. How symbolic!

Many towns decorate their streets with illuminated greens. The lamp poles are bedecked with stars, large candy canes or Christmas trees — all very gay and festive.

Let us all, as Tiny Tim said, "God bless everyone," and be merry at this wonderful time of the year!

Christmas in Germany

by Friderike Zweig

In German-speaking countries December, starting on the sixth of the month, is the time for Christmas celebrations. On this day St. Nicholas, intimately addressed as Nikolo, is expected to do all the nice things which Santa Claus does for American children later that month. The patron of good children, he is accompanied by a black fellow, the *Krampus,* a devilish-looking person with a long red tongue and a big tail, with a wooden basket on his back and noisy chains to frighten naughty children, threatening to put them into his basket and carry them off. In contrast, Nikolo's sack is full of presents and sweetmeats. His saintly attitude, bishop's garments and staff are most assuring.

These two knock at every door to fulfil their respective duties. Their likenesses can be bought at candy stores, where Nikolo's is made of sugar and gingerbread and the *Krampus's* of dried prunes.

This is also the time of the Christmas Fairs, where at the many booths in market squares one can buy toys, children's garments, candies, the many varieties of Christmas-tree trimmings and, above all, the figures and objects of the Christmas Crib — the little Jesus and his parents, the animals, the Three Wise Men, the shepherds, everything needed to re-create the holy scene from which the Nativity and mystery plays sprang and still survive staged in front of churches.

Nikolo, whose name stands for the celebration of the sixth of December, is not forgotten when Christmas preparations are started. Though Christmas trees of all sizes are in the squares and streets for all to see and buy, Christmas gifts are kept out of sight in the homes, and both children and grownups eagerly await the many surprise gifts that will gladden their hearts on Christmas Eve.

The Holy Night, the Eve of Christmas, December 24, is the culmination of celebrations starting at dawn in many small towns and villages, where there has been a revival of the old custom of *Weihnachtsblasen,* or "Christmas blowing," usually performed on a hill or a high point of the town to be heard for miles around. The tunes are usually old carols, the brass instruments timeless. In the country, weather permitting, there is, of course, sleigh driving over the snow-covered roads and through wintry forests. The sleighs, usually very old and many beautifully carved, are drawn by horses gaily decorated with chains and silvery, tinkling bells. Christmas Eve ends with the Midnight Mass in the parochial church or cathedral, followed by Christmas Day and St. Stephen's Day, December 25 and 26, respectively.

Soon after dawn on December 24 the door of the room where the Christmas tree stands and the distribution of gifts will take place is locked to all except the grownups who trim the tree with wax candles, gilded nuts, little red-cheeked apples, candies wrapped in gaily-colored papers, glass decorations, chains, angels' hair and, in many families, Christmas cookies baked in special molds.

In religious homes the most prominent place in the room is graced by the crib, large or small, made of paper, wax or wood and often beautifully carved. The set of figures is carefully kept year after year and passed on from one generation to the next, rivaling the large cribs seen in churches everywhere. The little child Jesus, called *Jesulein* or *Christkind* (Christ child), is, of course the center of the scene in the crib straw. Sometimes his blond curly head, with wings attached, can be seen on top of the Christmas tree, as if He would rest in his flight to children with his presents for them. The Christ child is said to be accompanied by a white-bearded man who has some outward similarity to Santa Claus but is of lesser importance — *Knecht Ruprecht*, Rupert the servant, the Christ child's carrier of presents too heavy for the holy child to carry and which are left under the Christmas tree before its candles are lighted.

Dinner of many special dishes for the evening after a day of fasting has been prepared in advance.

There are a few old-time rural superstitions attached to this day, one concerning unmarried women, who are said to receive a prophecy regarding their future husbands.

Christmas trees are not of Christian origin, having been taken over from the heathens. Just as churches were built over the ruins of ancient temples, these formerly pagan trees are covered with holy emblems.

Christmas carols are sung wherever a Christmas tree is to be found. One of these carols, originating on the border of Austria and Germany in the rural town of Oberndorf, is sung the whole world over — "Silent Night, Holy Night," by Joseph Mohr (1792-1848). One of his descendants is choir-master in the Cathedral of Salzburg, the Austrian town where the great Mozart was born, not far from little Oberndorf. Salzburg is famous for its annual festival and revival of mystic plays in the foreground of the cathedral. The Oberammergau *Passionsspiele* in nearby Bavaria are of earlier origin.

The Nativity was frequently a subject for the old German painters like Martin Schongauer, Duerer, Lucas Cranach, Mathias Gruenewald, the masters of the *Andachtsstil* or "Adoration style." The adoration of the shepherds and the Magi has always been a popular theme in poetry; in addition to folk songs with Christmas themes there are many old German poems as early as the fifteenth century and later including the classicists' works that have been set to music by great composers. Goethe's "Epiphanias," a humorous ballad, is one of the favorites.

It is quite usual in Germany and Austria for the snow to whiten the trees and rooftops and cover the streets and squares at Christmastime, making a winter festival of the holy day.

Not so many centuries ago, December 24 was regarded as the first day of the new year, a symbol that time could only be recognized in relation to the birth of Christ. Postponing the new year a week does not change this meanings of a new era. Christmas is the high point of hopes, the celebration of peace, for Jesus is looked upon as the Prince of Peace. Let us not, in any country of the world, forget His great message and words: *I am come to cast fire on the earth and what will I but that it be kindled* (LUKE 12:49).

Christmas in England

by Heather Harrison

MERRIE olde England is the soil in which Christmas took its first and firmest root; there for centuries Christmas has been a day of good cheer, thanksgiving and rejoicing. The spirit of good will to all men, joviality and merrymaking has its origin in England's earliest history, dimly discerned, when the banquet was given in honor of ancient gods and goddesses. When the Christians came to celebrate it, even the puritanism of the Anglo-Saxon was unequal to the task of defending the yuletide against the inroads of pagan rites and customs. Their early festivals coincided with the pagan ones that took place during the winter solstice, the turning point of the year when the days lengthened and grew warmer.

Many of the customs that charm us today are survivals of ancient druidic worship. Holly and mistletoe, even the Christmas carol, had their significance then, their symbolism and the superstitions concerning them persisting to the present time. Mistletoe has always been regarded as a sovereign remedy for all ills. Holly, too, supposedly has mysterious powers; planted near home, it was said to ward off witches and protect the occupants from severe weather. The Druids, an organized cast of priests, believed the holly's eternally green leaves proved that the sun never really deserted the earth. They regarded them as sacred. The spirit of the holly tree kept its beauty all year, keeping the world still attractive when the sacred oaks were bare of leaves. The Christians used evergreens extensively from pagan times as the emblem of eternal life. Greens are used to emphasize the Nativity idea, and the Christmas wreath originated from Christ's crown of thorns.

In the primitive festivals conducted by the Druids in the forests of England during the winter solstice, the mistletoe because of its growth in the sacred oaks was considered an object of veneration as well as a heaven-sent antidote to poison and a symbol of fertility. Solemn processions, all clad in white and wearing sprigs of holly in their hair, marched to the groves of oaks, bards, deviners, poets, priests and the prince of Druids, in their wake. Taking a knife from the herald, carried by bearers, the prince climbed the tree and cut down clumps of mistletoe which were caught in white mantels held by groups of young priests and small sprigs distributed to be hung over the entrances of houses.

In the Christian period Christmas carols were given new birth as the purified and exalted form of the hymns of the Saturnalia, the festivals in honor of Saturn, god of agriculture, held in Rome during the winter solstice. In modern times, carol singing on Christmas Eve is in vogue all over

England and in the east end of London. Older members of church choirs and Sunday school children parade the streets after midnight, singing outside the houses of the more influential parishioners. They are often invited into the dwellings and served tea, but more often given money. Carols often are sung outside the homes of England several days before Christmas.

Not all carols are religious in nature; they may be lively secular airs, convivial and love songs and merry ballads of questionable propriety, too. Dancing sometimes accompanies them.

The Christmas tree, which had been known in Germany some two hundred years before Queen Victoria married a German prince, appeared in England at that time, blazing with colored tapers, which to the pagans were symbolic of the return of the sun to the earth and which to the Christians of Christ is the light of their lives.

Christmas, the most democratic of all festivals, characterized by good will to all men, has been celebrated in the castles and great homes of England in a spirit of brotherhood. All classes joined in its merriment. The English country gentleman of the fifteenth and sixteenth centuries held open house; at daybreak on Christmas morning, servants and neighbors thronged the hall. The ale was broached, and blackjacks and Cheshire cheese with toast, sugar and nutmeg were plentiful.

During the reign of Queen Victoria, the lord of the manor and the country squire gave bountifully of their hospitality. Neighbors and their children from nearby farms and cottages and the household staffs were invited to enjoy the tree which was hung with fruit and presents, labeled with their names; paper caps and aprons were worn, crackers were pulled, whistles were blown and accordians played. Generally the celebrations terminated with the hymn, "Hark, the Herald Angels," followed by "God Save the Queen!"

In the twentieth century with its turmoil and uncertainties Christmas comes as a pause for good will and a dedication to the peace for whose blessings we pray. A modern squire, imbued with the spirit of his brothers throughout the still flight of centuries, pours out his blessings to his humble and opulent neighbors alike. He and his wife distribute gifts chosen carefully for every child in the neighborhood at the festivities in the manor house. The tree is gay with the colored electric lights which have taken the place of the flaming tapers. They will make wassail from a bowl containing hot, spiced ale, which the host will heat with sizzling pokers made red in the bright glow of the yule log's embers. The bowl is no longer the mighty wooden wassail bowl of old, but the logs in the fire are of sturdy oak — so redolent of yesterday's picturesque ceremony of the yule log, the log then a massive, frequently rugged, grotesquely-marked root of an oak drawn in triumph from its resting place on Christmas Eve.

With their presents, the guests each receive a slice of Christmas cake, trimmed smartly with sprigs of shiny holly leaves, the emblems of eternal life. Politely, they curtsy to their gracious host and hostess, and, grateful for their many kindnesses, they continue this practice when they pass them in the village streets.

The Christmas dinner, descended from the pagan feasts in ancient England and the great Christmas feasts of medieval times, retains many of its customs to this very day, though the bringing of the boar's head is missing today. For centuries it was placed at the head of the table as the master cook's initial dish, preceded by trumpeters and huntsmen with boar spears and drawn falchions. The head, born aloft by pages, had been garlanded and garnished with rosemary and laurel, and a lemon was placed in its grinning chops.

Quantities of food are not consumed today as they were in the Middle Ages, the heyday of the Christmas festival, when folks dined on peacocks, heron, capons, venison, mutton and brawn, as well as "yule doughs" and sweetmeats. But the English people have enjoyed the blessing of the mince pie at their Christmas dinners for well-nigh five centuries, the first made of chopped mutton, and later of minced partridge enclosed in a rich pastry. Gradually other ingredients found their way into these pies until they finally appeared in their present form of chopped meat, suet, sugar, apples, raisins, currants, citron, cloves and nutmeg. The best of luck is said to result from eating mince pie before Twelfth Night. Pies left over at the end of the season in the big houses are distributed to the poor.

The unique and highly-praised regional cooking of England has contributed to the beloved Christmas feast the plum pudding which rich and poor enjoy alike. Originally it was served at the first course of the Christmas dinner as a plum "pottage" with the best meats. Gradually it evolved into a sweet, stiff pudding, served as a dessert. Later, in the eighteenth century, it was named "plum pudding," "plum" meaning to rise or swell, as it did with the swelling of the raisins added to the mixture.

All these delicious dishes are enjoyed even in the smallest homes. A coal miner's family in the remotest district rejoices together by the warm fire at five o'clock on Christmas Eve, when its festivities start. At the neat table covered with the traditional white damask cloth, the members of the family eat their pies and seed cakes and a luscious Christmas cake gay with the ubiquitous holly. The mistletoe is there, too; though it used to be hung in the kitchen, and any female standing under it could be kissed by any young man present who claimed the right, it now has invaded the parlor. Kissing under the mistletoe is undoubtedly an innocent survival from the Saturnalia of the Romans when riot and license were rampant.

Thus festivities, great and small, in every corner of England celebrate the most glorious event in history, when heaven met earth in the birth of Christ our Saviour. They are a part of the universal history of the race.

An Irish Christmas

by Patrick Mahony

IN every Irish village on Christmas Eve you will see a candle burning. It is burning to commemorate the wanderings of Mary and Joseph. In some villages the shopkeepers present their customers with candles for this purpose. Some Irish farmers will tell you that at midnight on Christmas Eve they have seen cattle go down on their knees!

Christmas is best-enjoyed in the country, in the midst of a farming community or in blessed Connemara — that district in the west of the Emerald Isle where a poet has said there can be no destination. There is only a pause here and there for the traveler, a pause to let the scenery woo the eyes.

In this devout part of Ireland, Christmas Eve is like a page out of the Scriptures. Here white-washed, thatched cottages are scattered over the hillsides or mountain slopes and blend in beautifully with the sea and bog and sky. Long before midnight you see the faithful carrying torches, making their way to the nearest church. The windows glow through the darkness while you hear the solemn strain of music blending with the chanting hymns.

You may hear hymns you have never heard before, some of them translated from the Irish, and hundreds of years old. Here is an example of Christmas Irishry:

> *Little Babe who art so great,*
> *Child so young, who art so old.*
> *In the manger small His room*
> *Whom no Heaven itself could hold.*
>
> *Father not more old than Thou,*
> *Mother younger, can it be.*
> *Older, younger, is the Son!*
> *Younger, older, She than He.*

LIBRARY
College of St. Francis
JOLIET, ILL.

How well I recall a Christmas I spent in an Irish cottage home and saw so clearly how deeply a tradition of simplicity is burned into the Irish heart. It forcibly illustrated to me that the spiritual, unworldly philosophy of life is the true Irish genius.

It was a godly night, this Christmas Eve, for the stars were out and nothing moved in the unbroken canopy of heaven as the family gathered to go to Mass. Being a Protestant, I was to be left alone, there being no church of my denomination in the district. We were sitting round the hearth, a peat fire smoldering in the grate, exhaling smoke which is the true perfume of Ireland. Everyone drank "porter" beer, "the wine of the country." My host sang heart-rending songs of emigration, lamentation and woe. One song had Irish words, a melodious piece which brought the beauty of a thousand years ago into that humble home.

Moved by the mood of the music, I quietly slipped outside. I felt I would prefer to hear the music in the pathos of the evening light. With the wet fragrance of the wind blowing on my forehead, I listened as I gazed on the barren, heather-colored hills and beyond the great waste of ice-green sea. Here in this land of Celtic legend, relics of stone, bronze and pottery are still picked up on the dunes. Round the circuit of the bay, ancient earthworks may still be seen, connected with little harbors. One of these cuts through the keen-edged rock to a little strand where I could dimly see two curragh boats moored.

I pictured to myself the ancient mummers, or rhymers, wearing the traditional pointed hats in days of old, making the Christmas rounds, carrying their torches and accepting the gratuities in the base money which Queen Elizabeth forced on the Irish people — one part of silver, three of brass!

I stood there musing as there came from the cottage the lovely strains of "Noel! Noel!" sung by one and all in a mixture of joyous voices.

Reverently, slowly, they were singing the words of adoration, and I felt a renewal of life within myself. They were singing the hymn in the true Christmas spirit, accenting the symbol of rebirth within us all.

Amid these majestic surroundings, Christmas took on a clearer meaning to me. I reminded myself of the many Christmases which had passed to consolidate the undying efforts to make Ireland the land of a united people.

"With this spirit of reverence," I said to myself, "may they ever be worthy of their newly-won liberty!"

Christmas and St. Nicholas's Day

by Suzanne Silvercruys Stevenson

M*erci, merci, St. Nicholas!"* Belgian children shout in the fireplace and up the chimney to thank St. Nicholas, whose name in English is Santa Claus, for his toys and gifts on the morning of December 6.

In Belgium, which is a small country of only eight million inhabitants, next to France, Holland and Germany, Santa Claus comes in the night between the fifth and sixth of December instead of on Christmas night, which you all know is December 25. The reason for this might well be that St. Nicholas has to be through with his jobs and travels in Belgium by that time so he can get to England and America and to the other countries where people are expecting him at Christmas.

Then, too, in Belgium, Santa Claus travels in a cart pulled by a slow donkey, not in a sleigh pulled by reindeer — probably because there is not much snow in Belgium and a sleigh would be useless. At times, even when he is in a hurry, he has been seen riding the donkey and carrying his gifts in a large sack on his back. In French, which is one of the two languages the people of Belgium speak (the other language is Flemish), one often hears tales of *"St. Nicholas et son ane"* — the *ane*, which is the French for donkey, is very important indeed. So on the night of December 5 the children prepare a pail of water, a bag of oats and some fresh carrots to feed the donkey so he can do his job better and faster.

When I was a little girl in Belgium a long, long time ago, I would try to stay awake to hear Santa Claus come down the chimney, and I know that on several occasions I heard the kaying of the donkey. It might have been a dream, but all the food I left for him was always gone when I came down on December 6, and often the donkey had left traces of his visit downstairs.

For Belgian children December 6 is *their* day; it is also St. Nicholas's feast day in the lithurgical calendar. Grownups do not receive presents on this day. They have to wait until New Year's Day.

So Christmas Day, December 25, which in Belgium is called *Noel*, is a religious day for Belgium children. Christmas originally was meant to commemorate the birthday of Jesus Christ, the day he was born nearly two thousand years ago in a stable in Bethlehem.

On that day the children in Belgium pray to the infant Jesus for his help and guidance; they go to church with their parents and admire the reproduction there of the scenes of the Nativity.

It is thrilling and a sign of being grown-up to be allowed to attend church at midnight. Then, upon returning home, it is great fun to be

permitted to sip a little of the hot red wine flavored with cinnamon and nibble a cookie, a *gougnol*, made in the shape of a baby in swaddling clothes.

Different countries have different habits and customs, and the lives of people are built around these habits, also called tradition, and it is important to keep these traditions for they are the soul and the spirit of a country.

Here in America we too have wonderful traditions and as Americans we should hold these traditions very preciously so as to keep alive the purpose and the spirit of our wonderful United States of America!

Christmas in Austria

by Rosa L. Sheldon

HAVING spent most of my childhood in Austria, I should like to recall with happy memories Christmas at home in Vienna. There have been so many speculations about its origin it is best to say that mystery blurs the true answer.

In the eighteenth century the Christmas tree was fully ornamented and had wandered far and wide through the hamlets and towns of Germany. Around 1815 a German princess of Nassau Weilburg visiting the royal house of Habsburg introduced the *Weihnachtsbaum* to Emperor Franz Joseph I, who eagerly adopted this lovely custom, and the *Christbaum* has filled many a heart with the season's warm spirit ever since.

The month of December was always regarded as the most exciting month, anxiously awaited by young and old alike. In true Austrian tradition, Christmas Eve was celebrated on the twenty-fourth throughout the country. There was always lots of snow, and the buildings and busy market places with their proud, historical monuments, statues and fountains all stood clad in white. As evening approached, everyone hurried home with their last shopping; it felt good to be home with one's family.

The house was ready for the coming festivities. The chandeliers sparkled especially and were reflected in the polished windows and on parquet floors. The dinner table was set with white linen and gleaming crystal goblets. Silver that had belonged to many ancestors was used for this occasion. The mysterious aroma of a simple but delicious meal was the order of the day—hors d'oeuvres, fish of many kinds and salads. My favorite was a dessert of varieties of dried fruits, cut up, well seasoned and soaked in brandy, resembling a plum pudding, and served with *schlagobers* in individual cups.

After coffee, which followed, we would join our parents in the living room where the Christmas tree in all its glittering splendor was waiting for us. The piano was being played, and we all accompanied the old, well-known "Silent Night." After receiving our presents, we would sit and listen

to the beautiful Christmas poems father had selected. The evening would continue with the warm glow of candles and the lovely scent of a pine tree mingled with so many childhood dreams which are never quite forgotten.

The next day we would be off to Grandmother's house and spend the rest of our Christmas vacation with her. Those were happy days. As soon as we arrived by train at the *Bahnhof* in Graz, which was half a day's journey from home, there was Grandmother waiting for us with her sleigh drawn by black horses. Her gray-bearded groom would wrap and tuck us in with a great big furry blanket.

Off we'd go past fields and country roads where huge giant pine trees, heavily laden with snow, would nod a gentle welcome. Here and there one would see the footsteps of a deer that had gone through the forest looking for food or water. The shimmering icicles would dangle from many a branch and add to the beauty and mystery of nature. Not a sound was heard as on we went to the tinkling of the horses' bells until we reached Grandmother's house, where our presents were waiting under her tree and a wonderful Christmas dinner was being served. There was roast goose, spiced venison, pork and her own smoked ham and sausages and wine, not to forget varieties of baked goodies that were prepared many months ahead —a meal fit for a king.

In the late afternoon the grownups would join us children, and we would entertain with roasted chestnuts, cookies and heated wine new in season. Stories of long ago would be told until we children felt overcome by drowsiness under the spell of Christmas. Outside, the snow would glisten under the midnight sky, with millions of stars shining over a sleepy world, and the bells of St. Stephen would carry many a message over the partially frozen Danube to the far mountains with their proud and icy peaks, into the next dawn.

Christmas Days in Other Lands

by Lady May Lawford

CHRISTMAS is both the most liked and most disliked time of the year. Really, to enjoy Christmas one must be very young and possess the digestion of an ostrich—no ordinary one will do.

I spent the noisiest Christmas of my life in Honolulu. The Christmas dinner hour there is 5 P.M. in hotels and all restaurants as well as in the homes. From that hour until the following morning the time is given over to noise. The Chinese take a hand—why, I have no idea—letting off those earsplitting firecrackers as they do at their own Chinese New Year. These millions of firecrackers, pop-popping all night till dawn appears, making it "bad joss" to pop them any more, together with the trumpets and various instruments of noise used by many hundreds of roving revelers, make night hideous. Cars often are set afire by children throwing crackers, and if you do not put out your lights and lock your doors you let yourself in for a party that will cost you a nice bit of money for people you never saw before and probably never will see again!

Yes, Christmas in that gold-and-green paradise in the Pacific is very rough and noisy. They are quite mad on decorations there, and outside most houses you will find trees festooned with hundreds of colored lights or painted white, leaves and all, to imitate snow (although a quarter of the inhabitants have never seen snow, and ice only in cubes in the refrigerators!).

Quantities of inexpensive Christmas presents are exchanged; even the hotel servants come up and ask cheerily, "Where my Christmas present? You no got one for me?"

No, there is no beating about the bush out there!

AUSTRALIA is also a place where Christmas seems a little out of place. Intensely hot, blazing sun and dust in the clouds—and yet at the Christmas dinner hour at midday the sturdy Australian will eat traditional roast beef, Yorkshire pudding, turkey and as rich a Christmas pudding as you ever saw, followed by jam roll and custard and a large assortment of figs, nuts, prunes, dried fruits, etc. The afternoon is given over to rest, interspersed with occasional cups of tea and rich black plum cake!

Although they know little or nothing about it, the natives of India take a great interest in Christmas. They will decorate the house with masses

of colored paper, doll up the horses with marigolds in their ears and bring as "Clismas" present a sugar cake containing rose leaves. They all expect presents and are most anxious that master and mistress should enjoy their one fete of the year.

I shall never forget the last Christmas I spent in India. My dogs were decorated with ribbon bows on their tails and around their necks, their claws gilded with gold paint; my three horses had necklaces of marigolds, roses in their ears and red muslin rolled round their bridles till they looked like the bridegroom's horse at a native wedding. I had so many flowers they had to be placed in water jugs and pails, and the fruit was put in a carriage rug, which overflowed onto the carpet. It cost me a hundred rupees in "'backsheesh," but it was most gratifying to think back upon.

I have spent only one Christmas amid the correct setting of snow, pines, etc.; that was in the hills near Simla. The snow was so deep it was only possible to progress yards at a time. We arrived very late on Christmas Day at a rest house almost submerged in snow, with no fires to be had and very poor prospects of food. The day grew colder and colder. When I could stand it no longer, I sent for a chopper and chopped up a chair, a towel-horse and some curtain rails of the good, old-fashioned, thick kind and made a fire. Later on, my bearer arrived with a perfectly-cooked chicken, some dates and a half bottle of brandy, and that, with some hot boiled rice from the coolies' food, made up a most delicious Christmas dinner—aided by that valuable sauce, hunger!

Christmas in Ceylon, I remember, was most delightful. One year we spent it in the jungle and ate our dinner on the banks of a rice field. A great green-and-gold snake arrived, and no doubt wished us a merry Christmas in his own way, but it rather spoiled the party, and we fled in confusion.

Christmas on board ship is always fun, and I look back with pleasure on the many I have spent. It is better in the tropics because the sailor is a

hale-and-hearty soul who loves to live in a draft, shudders at the idea of central heating or shut doors and cannot imagine why anyone should feel cold if he does not!

THE most miserable Christmas I ever spent was on the Island of Majorca. We had an endless German Christmas dinner in one of the hotels: a suckling pig complete with orange in mouth was the highlight of the evening. After dinner some fresh-air fiend opened every door and window, and most of us retired to bed with terrific colds that lasted about three weeks. Having to pay for the paper hats and whistles on the dinner table so aroused the rage of an old Scotsman that he departed by the tripper-ship then in the harbor, entirely wasting his return ticket!

The Christmases I have most enjoyed were those spent at Cannes or Monte Carlo. The hotel keepers always excel themselves, and the chef works hard to produce a meal that will remain for years in one's memory.

In pre-depression days quite valuable presents were often given. On one occasion, at the table next to mine, a lady won a glorious diamond watch in a tombola.

One method of giving Christmas presents to guests was to put numbers on the dance floor; while the guests danced, a number was called and if you were lucky enough to be on it, you received a box of chocolates or a large bottle of perfume.

At those dinners we often saw someone of international interest—Mistinguett, the King of Sweden or the Baroness Orczy, to name but three.

One could not help enjoying Christmas in such a setting—the ballroom warm but ventilated and scented, the wines at supper as well chosen as the meal. And when the games of throwing little white balls at one another, beating the table with tiny springs or hammers and other follies began to pall, you could always take off to the local casino and perhaps win a really nice Christmas present.

White Christmas in Paris

by Count Francis G. de Szechenyi

CHILDREN, I will tell you a story you probably never heard.

Santa is the patron of all children. He crams the stockings with goodies for virtuous children or with bunches of birch rods for the naughty ones. There are a multitude of legends surrounding his name, indicating that he must have been a remarkable person, endowed with the quality of mercy and above all an abounding love for children.

Christmas Eve in France, especially in Paris, is a *fete*, the *reveillon*, a supper after midnight. The Christmas gifts, however, are given as *etrennes* to the children on New Year's Day.

In France, Christmas begins at a midnight mass in an ancient church. Everything is decorated in greens and beautifully illuminated. Sometimes after the mass all in attendance are invited to a hospitable French home. The menu card is a simple gift for monsieur and madame.

The celebration of *La fete des Rois*, Twelfth Night, is very amusing. In Paris most people prefer to go to a restaurant for this entertainment. The main food is a cake in which a bean, *la feve*, is hidden. When a man finds the bean, he shouts, "The king drinks!" All join in the toast to him, the king of the Twelfth Night, and he then chooses a queen. Should a woman find the bean, everybody salutes her, she shouts, "The queen drinks!" and she chooses her king. Then the king and queen direct their retinue to obey their whimsical commands.

I remember in Paris the streets were crowded and covered with snow. The beautiful shop windows were filled with toys, buzzing machines, talking dolls, etc. It was difficult to stay outside because of the icy blizzard. I rushed to my car, and I was able to reach the Opera where I was invited for the *reveillon*. Suddenly everything became silent—heavy snow covered the "Rose City."

That night I dreamed of Santa's shadow, speeding through the air in a golden reindeer sleigh . . . I dreamed of angels flashing in the holy blue night.

Christmas in Italy

by Josephine Garibaldi Ziluca

ONCE upon a time, many centuries ago, a child was born in Bethlehem. He was Jesus, our Lord and Saviour. He preached peace in all its meaning of love, joy, sacrifice, kindness, piety and understanding, and finally he gave his life on the Cross to uphold these principles so that we might enjoy in the years to come what he preached.

So it is that through the ages all over the world for the love of Him everyone celebrates the day of his birth. In Italy we call the celebration *Natale*, the Feast of the Nativity.

It is a deeply religious festival; when paganism was still supreme 1959 years ago, it had to be celebrated in natural or excavated grottos, under the earth, in cireis called the *Catacombe*. In the deep of the night, shadows would disappear through the holes of the hidden entrances, their well-covered faces under their robes so no one could recognize them. Patricians, soldiers, slaves, old and young, women and children who had embraced the Christian faith, gathered together in the dim light of oil lamps in silent prayer and whispered chants, knowing well that if they were caught by the pagan soldiers they would be burned alive on crosses or thrown to the lions in the arenas.

But with the passing of centuries the Christian faith triumphed and the Feast of the Nativity could be celebrated in all its glory.

From the little villages high on the snowy Alps to the bustling cities of the plains, to the hamlets in the lovely orange groves in Sicily, as night falls on Christmas Eve thousands of churches, small and large, burst out in floods of light and music. All Italy is illuminated by thousands of candles, adorned by beautiful damasks embroidered in gold and silver and precious stones. In the churches red carpets cover the steps and aisles and flowers bedeck the altars. In the center of all this beauty on the main altar is a reproduction of the simple stable with the cows and donkeys, camels and sheep, the shepherds, the kings; and in the middle the manger where the baby Christ is laying, his beautiful and saintly mother near him and all the figures expressing deep devotion and wonder. This is the *Presepio*. The great artists Di La Problia, Michelangelo, Domatello, Sansovino and others created

most beautiful figurines of the scene. These are priceless treasures in our time and are shown just once a year on this occasion.

In the great cathedrals, as in the humble churches, a choir of children dressed in red cassocks and white surplices sing the glory of the Nativity; in the monasteries the nuns and the monks pray devotedly, chanting the litany; and the murmur of their prayers and the enchanting music of the organs and the children's voices fill the air of the silent night with untold joy.

After reunions of families over lovely dinners, the people flock to the churches, where at midnight the bells join in the music and a High Mass is celebrated. For a few minutes at the climax of the Mass the music stops and a great silence descends on earth, and in that silence all people, kneeling devoutly, promise to forgive all grievances so that peace will be supreme on the Nativity Day.

In the early morning hours of Christmas Day children find their stockings, hung on the fireplaces the night before, filled with presents if they are good, or with black coals if they are naughty. In addition to this celebration, in our time presents are added for adults and for children by the *Befana,* who takes the place of Santa Claus and descends the chimneys at night while they sleep. Christmas trees are a recent addition and are to be found only in the larger cities where people of foreign birth and traditions dwell.

But even now, wherever you go in Italy, at midnight for a few moments when the sound of the music and bells is stilled every street is deserted and an awing, joyous silence descends upon that land as if at that moment the Christ our Lord is reborn; and every head is bent in the joyous prayer: *"Gloria in Excelsis Deo!"*

Pedro's Posada—Christmas in Mexico

by Gladys and Ray Owen

PEDRO was awake long before he heard the maid's soft knock on his bedroom door. Since long before daylight he had been thinking of his visit to Queretaro where he was going to stay with his grandparents during the Christmas festivities (which in Mexico last for nine days, December 16-24, and are called the *Posadas*).

As he waited in bed for the maid to bring his hot chocolate and *pan dulce,* or sweet roll, he thought about the *Posadas* of last year. It was the custom of his village to celebrate the story told in the Bible of the journey of Mary and Joseph to Bethlehem on the nine nights before Christ was born. Each evening a procession was led by the children—the smaller ones in front, followed by their older sisters, brothers and parents. Last year Pedro had been big enough to carry the Virgin Mary which, with the figures of Joseph and an angel, led the procession. They marched from house to house, chanting litanies and special songs the parish priest had taught them for this Christmas season, each one in the procession carrying a lighted candle.

It was a beautiful sight to watch this group wind its way through the narrow cobblestone streets of the little village, knocking on doors and, in song, asking for shelter—for *posada* means lodging or shelter.

At each of the houses last year they were refused admittance until finally they came to the ninth house. Here, when those behind the locked door asked, "Who is there?" they replied, "It is the Queen of Heaven, who is seeking shelter." The great heavy wooden door was swung open for them to enter. They came into a large room, at one end of which figures were set up in the *nacimiento,* or manger. Everyone in the group knelt and prayed in front of the manger.

After prayers, refreshments were served and the *pinatas* were broken. (A *pinata* is a clay jar, usually in the form of an animal or bird, decorated with tissue paper of many colors. The jar is filled with small toys, coins, fruits, nuts and candies, which are also wrapped in gaily-colored paper. The *pinata* is usually hung by rope from the ceiling or balcony so that it can be raised or lowered by a grownup. Starting with the youngest, a child is blindfolded, turned three times around and given a stick with which he has three tries to break the *pinata*. The *pinata* is kept moving up and down, and the first child rarely succeeds in breaking it; but finally it is broken and there is a mad scramble for the shower of goodies which fall on the floor.)

Pedro particularly remembered the *pinata* he had broken last year. It was in the shape of a white bird with many colored streamers for feathers.

[41]

Pedro felt he was big enough then to have broken it by himself without the help of his Uncle José, who was handling the rope and had taken pity on him and kept the *pinata* still. He still had some small straw burros, souvenirs of this *pinata*.

But now it was time to get up. As he dressed he could hear the hustle and bustle of the servants as they took the suitcases to the courtyard in readiness for their departure for Queretaro. If he did not hurry he would be left behind.

The trip to Queretaro took several hours, but it did not seem long to Pedro. The road was crowded with others on their way to the big city for the festivities. There were many family groups like Pedro's, as well as chickens, turkeys and pigs, and burros loaded with charcoal and food being driven to the city market.

Grandfather's house in Queretaro was near the principal *plaza*, or main square. The rather plain, fortress-like walls, whose windows were covered with heavy iron grillwork, gave no hint of the beautiful *patio*, or courtyard, of the living quarters inside. In the center of the main *patio* was a fountain which dated back to the time of Cortez, for Grandfather's family had been one of the first Spanish families to settle in Mexico. Large poinsettias were in bloom around the *patio*. Their beautiful red flowers are so much a part of the Christmas season Mexicans call them the *flor de Noche-buena,* or the Christmas-Eve flower.

The walls of the *patio* were covered with red and purple bougainvillaea, and along one sunny wall was a large cage filled with brightly-colored small songbirds. On his perch off to one side was Grandmother's green parrot. No one knew his age exactly, but he was much older than Pedro. The boy considered him very wise because he could sing and talk, and so he greeted him respectfully. Then he hurried on with his family to greet his grandparents and the many relatives who had come for the *Posadas.*

December 16 came quickly and brought the first of the *Posadas* Pedro had been looking forward to. This time, instead of going from house to house, the procession stayed inside Grandfather's large *patio*. All the guests took part, and Grandmother had "angel" costumes made for her little grandchildren. Each night the ninth door they knocked on, which opened to admit them, led the guests into the room where the Nativity scene was set out. This beautiful scene was much more elaborate than any of those in his village. Even the little town of Bethlehem was completely represented with small houses, trees and even a river emptying into a small lake. The streets were cobblestoned, just as in Pedro's village. There were figures of townspeople and animals on the streets and shepherds with their flocks of sheep on the hills. For many years Grandmother had been collecting these beautifully-carved figures in village market places where the skilled wood carvers displayed their wares.

On Christmas Eve the figures of Mary and Joseph were put in their proper places, and then Aunt Maria and Uncle Miguel brought in the figure of the Christ child, which they tenderly placed in the manger. It was a most impressive scene, and they all knelt before the manger in prayer.

After the prayers, Pedro went with the older members of the family to the big cathedral for the Midnight Mass. On the way they saw, being carried through the streets, many floats representing biblical scenes. They were beautifully made and had taken their owners many months of hard work to complete.

When they returned home, the family had the traditional supper with many special and delicious dishes. They exchanged a few gifts, though most of the presents were kept for January 6, the day in Mexico and in many other countries when children receive gifts and toys—not from Santa Claus but from the Three Kings, the *Santos Reyes.*

Before Pedro and his sisters and cousins went to bed on the evening of January 5, they put their shoes in the balcony windows of their bedrooms. In these shoes were letters they had written to the Three Kings, asking for toys and gifts. Since the Three Kings brought gifts to the Christ child, the children believed that the Three Kings would bring gifts to them, too.

Early the next morning the children hunted for the gifts and toys which had been left for them. Pedro was given almost everything he had asked for, and his sisters and cousins, too, were very pleased with their numerous gifts.

That evening Grandfather gave a party for his family and their good friends and neighbors. Pedro was allowed to stay up until after the *rosca de Reyes,* a crown-shaped cake sprinkled with sugar on top, was served with hot chocolate. As is almost everything in Mexico, this custom is a blend of the Spanish and the Indian, for the cake is Spanish and the drink Indian. Pedro was finishing his refreshments when there was sudden excitement where his parents were seated—there was a tiny porcelain doll in his father's piece of cake. It had been mixed in the batter and baked in the cake. In Mexico it is the custom that whoever finds the little doll in his piece of cake must give a party very soon and invite all who were present when the doll was found.

Pedro went to bed that night tired but very happy, for he knew that he was soon to be invited to another party.

Christmas Celebrations in Guatemala

by Gerda de Topke

THE world has grown so small as a result of distance-destroying inventions that Christmas has become a universal celebration; this very special feast at the end of each year has more than a Christian significance. It is as old as the conscience of the human mind, going back into the darkest ages when man first began to realize how much he depended on changes in weather and therefore on seasons.

The origin of this custom was in the Northern Hemisphere. The inhabitants of regions there began to observe that the sun was most important in their daily lives. The winter solstice, at the end of December, meant the return of warmer weather and more comfort. At the same time the discovery of fire was closely associated with the light and warmth of our guiding star, the sun. This is why we always find fire, light, candles and warmth intimately connected with this most important of all festivities in the life of the human community.

It is not a coincidence that Christmas is also closely related to the climate where it is celebrated—and this brings us to Central America.

Somehow the spirit of a festival has to have its preparation in the mind of man. In Europe we find the celebrations of St. Nicholas in Holland, the Advent Sundays in Germany and other local customs in the various northern countries. In Guatemala, Mexico and Central America it is the *Posada*, the seeking of shelter, referring to the travel of Joseph and his wife Mary toward Bethlehem for the census. According to tradition, they had a hard time getting a place to stay and finally had to share their shelter with an ox and an ass in a tavern stable. The *Posada* re-enacts this in detail in nine days— nine being a holy number in the questions of the human soul. Before Christmas you will hear the beat of the turtle shells (turtles are a cornflour dough around pork flavored with hot red peppers and wrapped in banana leaves) announcing that a procession carrying Joseph and Mary through the streets is seeking a house where shelter will be given to this eternal pair of wanderers. Each night the group will seek another home, singing one of the many traditional melodies (these have mostly not been recorded and are handed down verbally) and asking for shelter—to be rejected first and then finally accepted wtih rejoicing, in the hope that this home giving hospitality to the holy couple will be blessed by their presence.

Then each house will treat their guests to *punche*, a warm drink made of tea with dried fruits and cinnamon and sometimes spiced with rum. This beverage is most welcome, for even in the tropics the nights at the end of the year can be cold.

[45]

The last night is Christmas Eve, and the house receiving the *Posada* on this occasion is the most blessed and prepares the elaborate festival of the crèche, or *Nacimiento* (also called the *Pesebre*, according to an old Italian tradition).

The *Nacimiento* is one of the most elaborate preparations for Christmas and Christ's birth. Many of the Catholic churches in Guatemala also make *Posadas*, wandering from one church to another, asking the parishioners to join in the journey. They will construct a *Nacimiento* based on the old Italian paintings depicting Christ's birth in a wonderful landscape. Also in private homes you can find a whole room given over to a crèche that sometimes take four to eight weeks to complete. It is often a replica of the landscape, its deep ravines and little thatched huts, the Indians creeping along the steep paths.

At the Christmas market, called the Shepherd Market (*Mercado de los Pastores o Pastorcitos*—the latter, little shepherds), you will find varieties of most attractive miniatures of every artifact of daily life in Guatemala. The market is typical of the admirable handicraft of the humble people of the country. You will find a pine cone changed into a strutting turkey, palm trees made out of tin, lifelike Indians in their colorful costumes arrayed on little cartons and the popular humor of the people expressed in their everyday weakness. The eye cannot catch all the subtle details in one visit; every time you visit the market you will discover a new masterpiece.

The mild climate is reflected in customs that would be impossible in the stern cold of the North. A special custom is the *pinata*, in which an earthen pot filled with candy and surprises is first elaborately transformed into a huge pineapple and then is shattered when a blindfolded person strikes it with a stick. This custom is generally confined to birthday parties for children. The *pinata* emphasizes again the skillful hands of the people of Guatemala; almost any figure in a *pinata* can be obtained.

On Christmas Eve the Midnight Mass is just as important as the *Posadas* which have placed the Christ child into the elaborately prepared *Nacimiento*. Christ has been born. The bells announce the happy event. Twelve o'clock comes, and with it the deafening sound of all types of firecrackers. the air will be filled with the odor of sulphur and smoke for a long time. The streets are alive with adults and children throwing their firecrackers into the midst of the traffic and tooting horns. Everybody gets to church, to be filled wtih the soothing moment of devotion. After then they all return to their homes to eat their tamales.

In all homes a few days after Christmas the *Novena del Nino* is started —nine days of praying for the Child Christ, for his protection of the home and for his experience of fleeing to Egypt. Most people end this prayer on Three Kings' Day with a festival similar to Christmas.

On New Year's Eve the Christ child is raised to a sitting position and is dressed in the daintiest clothes possible. The last day of the Novena is usually accompanied by the noise of rattles, called *chin-chines*, the beat of turtle shells and little earthen whistles. This is decidedly the old Indian tradition which was worked into the representation of Christ's birth by the Spanish missionaries.

Christmas Celebrations in Scandinavia

by Evelyn Peterson

SWEDEN

THE Christmas celebration in Sweden really begins on December 13, St. Lucia Day. On that day one of the daughters in each family chosen as St. Lucia dresses in a white dress with a red sash and wears a crown of lighted candles. She is an important figure in planning the family's Christmas festivities and her first duty that morning is to bring her family coffee and freshly-baked buns for breakfast in bed.

St. Lucia is a legendary figure representing innocence and virtue. Legend has it that in the early days of Christianity there lived in Sicily a lovely girl of seventeen named Lucia. She was betrothed and her family had consigned a large dowry. The day before the wedding, however, Lucia's mother became very ill. Lucia prayed to God, promising that if her mother was spared she would give the entire dowry to the poor. The mother recovered and Lucia was true to her promise. But her husband-to-be, furious and refusing to go through with the wedding, betrayed Lucia to the army, which in that time was persecuting the Christians, and poor Lucia was burned at the stake. Soon thereafter people began "seeing" Lucia here and there. She appeared in many places, always doing kind things for the underprivileged. In Sweden one bitterly cold night of December 13 centuries ago she is supposed to have appeared before hundreds of cold and hungry people. The Swedish people came to love Lucia, the "Queen of Light," as they called her, and December 13 has become the day marking the beginning of the Christmas season.

Christmas Eve is perhaps the most important period of the yule season. There is almost always snow on the ground when the members of the family gather for the thrilling evening of laughter and worship. They usually exchange gifts early in the evening and at eleven o'clock attend the midnight service at the church. Then they return home for a great feast, the most beautiful dinner of the year amid lovely table decorations and candles in brightly-colored candelabras. The dinner traditionally features a popular dish known as *lute-fisk*. After dinner they sing carols around the Christmas tree, and the children are permitted to stay up as late as they like on this wonderful night.

There is no Santa Claus in Sweden, but, rather, a merry old gentleman known as the *Tomte-guben* who looks very much like our Santa. He neither comes by sleigh nor slides down chimneys; instead, he just appears from

nowhere on Christmas Eve with a sack of presents on his back for the children.

On Christmas morning at six everyone goes to an early church service known as *Jul-otta*. The church is beautifully lighted with candles, and the music drifts out over the snow as the people approach the church. After the service they remain to have coffee together and exchange greetings. Then they return to their homes—some to take a long nap, others to visit and still others to begin preparations for the big dinner which is the highlight of Christmas Day.

DENMARK

Christmas Eve marks the beginning of the Danish yule observance. Work ceases in the afternoon and at five o'clock church bells in town and country begin to chime to summon people to worship in candle-lit churches decorated in green. After the service the families hasten to their homes for a magnificent feast.

The selection of a Christmas tree is an important family rite. Hans Christian Andersen in his tale *The Fir Tree* tells how the tree is selected in the woods and brought inside as a Christmas guest in every Danish home as well as in the hotels and shops. Actually, the tree as a symbol of Christmas is relatively recent throughout Scandinavia, having been introduced from Alsace early in the nineteenth century.

The traditional Christmas Eve dinner begins with rice porridge sprinkled with cinnamon. Whoever gets the almond hidden in the porridge receives a prize. Next comes roast goose stuffed with apples and prunes and served wtih red cabbage and small browned potatoes. The dessert is often apple cake topped with whipped cream.

After dinner—if there are children in the home—father and mother disappear into a locked room, light the tree there and then throw open the doors as the children gape with open-mouthed wonder at the beautifully-decorated Christmas tree which has been concealed from them until this moment. Around the foot of the tree are the gifts wrapped in gay papers. It is a Danish custom for all to take one another by the hand and dance around the tree, singing old Danish Christmas hymns.

Sometimes the gifts are not under the tree but are distributed by *Nisse*, who is somewhat equivalent to our Santa Claus. *Nisse* is a sprite, very popular in Danish folklore, who does all sorts of mischief, though he is friendly and lovable in his long white beard and red cap.

Denmark is usually covered with snow at Christmas time, and it is customary to put out bread and grains for the birds. The farmers always save fine sheaves of grain at harvest time, and at Christmas place them on high poles for the birds.

A favorite Christmas story book for children is one called *Peter's Jul*. The drawings are simple and charming, and the natural verses tell of the joy and glory of Christmas.

[50]

NORWAY

THE approach of Christmas is marked in Norway by a thorough house-cleaning and a great flurry of cooking and baking. On Christmas Eve all work must be finished by four in the afternoon, when the village church bell rings in the Christmas season. Then the families assemble for Christmas Eve celebrations in their homes. In most regions the dinner starts with a bowl of rice porridge. One of the bowls contains an almond, and there is something good in store for the finder, it is said. *Lute-fisk* or perhaps pork cutlets or boiled codfish is the main dish of the feast.

Following the dinner the scene moves to the living room where the Christmas tree stands brightly decorated. Before trees became the symbol of Christmas in the mid-nineteenth century, it was customary for every home to feature a yule log which burned and smoldered all through the holiday season.

Until recently Norway had no Santa Claus tradition. Gifts generally were handed out by the head of the family. But in recent years the popularity of St. Nick in England and Santa Claus in the United States has led to the resurrection of the ancient Norse figure *Julenisse*, a mythical sprite who is particularly popular with children. After the gifts have been distributed, young and old join hands and circle around the decorated tree, singing Christmas carols.

Norway celebrates fourteen days of Christmas. On December 25, the "First Day of Christmas," Norwegians rise early for church services, after which they visit and exchange greetings. The first two days of Christmas are mainly family affairs, but on the remaining days there is much visiting with friends and neighbors. In some areas one is expected to call on each of his neighbors, who is supposed to maintain a table of delicacies for the guests. In many parts of the country it is a "must" to have fourteen different kinds of cookies on hand—a different kind for each day of the yule celebration.

Parties, visits and general celebration continue to New Year's Day—a particularly festive day, and on through January 6, "The Day of the Three Wise Men."

As in every country, the end of the season is greeted with some sadness but with happy thoughts of other Christmases to come.

The Real Santa Claus

by Oguz R. Turkkan

A FEW years ago, Americans read with some surprise that Santa Claus was born in Turkey. Since this claim appeared in Ripley's "Believe it or Not!" series, they did not know what to believe. How could the red-cheeked, crimson-clad jolly old fellow from the North Pole, with all his reindeer and sleigh and snow, actually come all the way from Turkey!

Unbelievable though it sounds, it is true. Of course, the real Santa Claus did not have a sleigh or the companionship of Rudolph, the red-nosed reindeer—and neither was Turkey called Turkey then. And he would have been mighty uncomfortable wearing that heavy furred costume in Antalya, his home town. But in kindness of heart and willingness to help, the real Santa Claus was as good as his legendary twentieth-century symbol. His life story is a wonderful one and the spread of his fame from South to North is similarly amazing.

Firstly, he was not called Santa Claus. His real name was St. Nicholas, but the Dutch, when they learned about him, corrupted his name to "Claus," and he "migrated" with the Dutch to America under this name. Since we now know and cherish him by this nickname, let's continue to call him Santa Claus.

Let's visit his first home. Today we'd take a plane or ship to the Eastern Mediterranean country of Turkey, landing in fabulous Istanbul (formerly Constantinople), and then overland to the southern tip of Turkey, to the Gulf of Antalya, named after its most famous city. The region is beautiful —like France's Riviera—blue waters, orange groves, palm trees, silky blue skies and, for a surprising background, snow-covered mountains!

Near Antalya, in a city called Patara, Father Christmas was born, and it was in the neighboring town of Myra (now Demre) that he lived and died as bishop. His church and some of his remains are still in Turkey (some of his bones were stolen and taken to Italy, in the first move that took his fame westward).

Legends claiming Santa Claus to be a miraculous saint arose right after his birth, which is placed late in the third century. Let's pass over these myths to come to the incident that started his fame as a good-hearted man:

When Santa was a young man in Patara, he had a noble but impoverished neighbor with three daughters. The girls were of marriageable age, but who would marry a maid without a dowry? It simply was not done

[52]

in those days—at least not by self-respecting gentlemen! However, the girls were more concerned about their father, who was taking his family's lowered status very hard, than about their own misfortune. They debated the best way to help him. Each sister was willing to sacrifice herself in the slave market to pay off her father's debts, but neither would allow the other to offer herself at auction. They could reach no decision, and fell into each other's arms and started to cry.

Santa Claus wanted to help, but without hurting the feelings of the nobleman, who would not take charity. He already had learned that the best help is given secretly, anonymously, and he had developed quite a technique—he spied on those in deep desperation, as they turned to God in prayer, and he would toss a purse full of gold coins to them through the chimney or the open windows. (He was, of course, assisted in the fact that he had some money, and the semi-tropical climate of this region made closed windows unknown!)

Santa decided to do the same thing for his neighbor. On a still December night—just like the night when the stars shone down on Bethlehem, one of those silent nights when, with some imagination, you can hear the angels sing—Santa was waiting. Through the cracks in the roof to which he had climbed, he watched as the old man prayed and wept silently. Santa sent his gold-filled purse down the chimney and ran away as nimbly as a skilled robber. He could hear the poor man's surprised thanks to God: "Thou hast indeed heard my prayers!"

Santa felt lighthearted and happy in the thought that the greatest fun of all could be had by secretly helping those in need. He vowed to make this an avocation.

The story—part myth, part truth—goes on to tell us how Santa Claus, discovering that he did not put enough gold in the purse, tried twice more to repeat his trick on his neighbor. But in the last try the nobleman grabbed him in the night by his red tunic. Santa hid his face and pleaded with the man to let him go and never try to find out whether he was an angel or a human being. Finally he wrenched himself free of the old man and ran away, but a piece of his red tunic remained in the grasp of the nobleman, and everyone knew who the benefactor was. Respecting Santa's wishes, however, everyone pretended not to know and attributed the three purses to an angel. That is why today, at Christmas, when you find your present in your stocking, you suspect who put it there, but you pretend that a particular angel, Santa Claus, visited your house that night. Indeed, giving gifts in secret and as a surprise is the true fun of giving and the true spirit of Christmas.

The story of the three purses gave birth to another custom—the three golden balls over pawnbrokers' doors, the emblem of their trade, represents the three purses of gold thrown by Santa Claus into his neighbor's house! The pawnbrokers of the Middle Ages always regarded themselves as saints, helping those in need by lending them money (for a profit, of course, but why raise that point here?). The story of Santa's generosity appealed to their sense of kinship with him, and they placed the sign of three purses atop their stores to make their business appear more dignified and brotherly.

To this day in Europe and in the United States, pawnbrokers always display that sign, though they may well have forgotten what it is supposed to signify.

Santa Claus finally became bishop of Myra, forty miles away from his home. Many miracles have been attributed to him, which explains why he was called a saint. Infants and children are usually the beneficiaries of his miraculous interventions. In one instance a forgetful mother left her baby in a tub of water over a fire. Then she remembered, and started running home; but Santa Claus had already prayed to God. The woman found the tub on the fire, the water in it boiling, and the baby in it—but alive and unhurt, playing merrily with the boiling bubbles!

Another myth puts Santa Claus in the rôle of Sherlock Holmes. When three school children are lost, he tracks down an innkeeper, investigates the house as thoroughly as a private eye and then falls to his knees and prays, whereupon strange movements begin in three large pickle barrels in the inn—the three students, who were killed, mutilated and hidden in the tubs by the innkeeper, come to life!

All the Santa Claus stories end with him forgiving even the most monstrous crimes, and the criminals, in their repentance, becoming pillars of the church, good men. That's the Christmas origin of "good will toward men."

Some of the stories of Santa Claus deal with sailors, which is quite natural since Myra was then an important coastal city. In one of these legends, Santa Claus is credited with stopping a raging storm on his pilgrimage to the Holy Land. This miracle spread his fame around the Mediterranean, and sailors adopted him as their saint (a few centuries later, admiring Italian sailors stole his bones from his burial place and took them to Italy).

And once, when famine struck Myra, he pleaded with visiting seamen to give part of the cargo grain on their ship to the starving people. The seamen refused until the insistent bishop promised them: "You cannot suffer for doing a good deed." The sailors could not deny their patron saint, and they opened the hatches. As the grain poured down, they noticed a miraculous thing—not a pound of their cargo diminished! When they left, their ship was as full of grain as before they gave it to the needy. Santa Claus had made his point—"You cannot suffer for doing a good deed."

Many other stories picture Santa Claus helping anyone in trouble, but especially eager to help children and be with them. Thus the marble of his sarcophagus has but two carved figures: two reclining children. Even in death, Santa Claus wanted the company of the children he loved so dearly.

His death is given as December 6, 342 A.D. The church in which he used to preach and in which he was buried still stands in Myra (Demre). After his death the Church of Santa Claus became a shrine, and pilgrims from all over the Mediterranean came to visit it.

In 1087 some Italian sailors or merchants came to Myra, waited until the three monks guarding the tomb were asleep and then broke the marble sarcophagus and stole the relics of the saint. In their hurry they overlooked two of Santa's bones, which are now on display at the Museum of Antalya. The Italians carried these remains to Bari, in southern Italy, where they built a church to house them. The church still stands and is the European center of the cult of St. Nicholas.

His fame spread throughout Western Europe. He became a patron saint in Greece, Germany, Austria, Belgium, the Netherlands, France and parts of southern and northern Italy. The Russians jumped on the bandwagon, too, and declared Santa Claus the chief patron saint of all Russia.

Some accepted him as the patron of children and youth, some of scholars, others of seamen and river boatmen.

It is interesting to note that in England the Santa Claus festivities originally started on December 6, the day of the death of the historic St. Nicholas. As the Santa Claus festivities extended into the Christmas season, the Christmas spirit covered them and the two observances merged into one, with Santa Claus becoming a Christmas character.

And how did St. Nicholas of Turkey conquer America? The festival of Santa Claus was very popular in Holland, and when the Dutch came to America and founded Niew Amsterdam (now New York), they brought the festival with them. The first immigrant boat that touched Manhattan Island is reported to have had the figurehead of the saint on its bow. Santa became the patron saint of Niew Amsterdam. Soon his festival spread all over the new land as part of the Christmas celebration. By that time, after moving that much north, it was natural for the now Dutch-looking saint to have a jolly, Nordic appearance and drive his reindeer in from the polar regions.

He is now, more than ever, the true spirit of the joy of giving and of good will and peace among people everywhere.

Rex Miller, an American who went in search of Santa Claus in Turkey and did a good detective job, ends his book *In Search of Santa Claus:*

> Americans who go in search of the true Santa Claus will discover that their trail leads them through Europe into Turkey. There they will find a warm welcome from a hospitable, friendly people who are today linked with the Western world by ties of common interest and mutual esteem.

A Turkish proverb reflects the true spirit of Santa Claus—to help for the joy of helping, without looking for thanks or gratitude. This is what the people of Turkey, from where Santa Claus came, love to repeat and to believe.

> *If you help, throw your name to the sea;*
> *If no one knows and no fish knows,*
> *God sure will know it, and you know it.*

The Star of Bethlehem
and the Gypsy Blacksmith

by Lars Eriksson Lind

EACH year, commemorating the Wise Men of old, Christendom scans the heavens anew for a reappearance of the star, hoping for peace on earth, and each year in the lowly cave of the inn is re-enacted by ceremony and effigy the advent of the Prince of Peace lying in a manger beside the star of Bethlehem.

When my parents took me out to Jerusalem, Palestine was a Turkish province where, except for a century of Crusader domination, Arab and Turk have stood guard over the most venerable shrines of Christendom and maintained the ownership intact for thirteen hundred years. Within these precincts, Mohammedan guards have kept vigil night and day to preserve the *status quo* and safeguard the time-established right of each sect from encroachment by the others. From this hub of Christian rivalry radiate its sectarian divisions, ever widening and separating as the wheel encircles the earth.

One of my earliest recollections is of our Mohammedan landlord, the aga of the *gendarmerie,* scarring whose kindly face were the ragged eyelids always watering over a glass eyeball replacing the one cut in two by a hatchet blow intended by one priest for another when this officer stepped in between to separate them. Yet he was never heard to malign or show revenge in the many succeeding years during which, as commander of the gendarmes, he was responsible for the maintenance of order during the Easter and Christmas ceremonies. In these impressionable years it was noble men such as he, the so-called "unbelievers," who strengthened that prophetic warning that men unknown and unnamed would come in "from east and from west and sit down . . ." while the "chosen" ones were left outside.

So tense did the religio-political situation become each year during the high festivals that the Turks followed the Roman pattern and carved out of the vast province of Syria the autonomous *sanjak* of Jerusalem with a governor reporting directly to the Sublime Porte in Constantinople, just as Pontius Pilate was directly responsible to Rome for approximately the same area at the time of Christ.

Growing up within sight of these sacred precincts, one became increasingly aware of the fact that he was treading literally in the footprints of the greatest lives ever lived, and that the Bible could be opened like a guidebook to many of these historic spots which no scholar has ever dis-

puted. The very road we trod was only a thin clay surface laid over the Roman stone bed. The street we traversed daily to school was the Roman road from Caesarea, from a fork of which, a mile or so north of Jerusalem, we had secured for our private museum the milestone placed there, as the Roman inscription told, during the reign of Augustus Caesar. A milestone which St. Paul must have passed on his way to the seaport and to Rome.

Taking our Bible history in this literal fashion, I recall vividly the first visit of our junior class to Bethlehem. Five miles over a rough macadam road in a horse-drawn wagon in those days took us nearly as long as it did the Wise Men on the selfsame route. But in the early spring, winding round those terraced hillsides of olive and vine and fig, aglow with myriads of bright crimson anemones, poppies, cyclamen and carpets of pink and yellow mustard, it was a sight none wished to hurry by, so striking in contrast to the Judean wilderness below toward the Dead Sea which had already been baked by the sun to the hue of camel's hair on the smooth hump-like hills. Yet the terraces and trees always remained to distinguish the "Little Town of Bethlehem" and lift it above all the hills. "The loveliest view in the Holy Land," Holman Hunt had once said, when standing at a viewpoint where, in later years, Lady Hunt set up a stone seat in his memory.

On the narrow cobbled streets of Bethlehem you could see many "Josephs" and "Marys." But it was usually Joseph who straddled the little ass while Mary walked behind, carrying the babe in a sling on her back, the round market basket on her head and the spindle twirling the yarn between her fingers.

Then the open square and, facing it, the oldest Christian church in the world built over the most famous of all inns and stables. The high, vaulted doorway of Queen Helena's time, which ushered in the Golden Era, had given way to a lower one as peace declined, and then to the present one— only a square needle's eye through which even rich men might enter by bowing very humbly and raising their heads cautiously. Feet of multitudes have deeply gouged the threshold, but only a gently rounded edge bespoke the impact of heads too impatient to rise from under the wide stone lintel above. At first sight, one sees just another Roman basilica but for the cross into which the apse has been transformed. Every nook is crammed with history from the five-hundred-year-old beams of English oak in the ceiling to the stone pavement beneath which lies the original mosaic floor, one of the finest in existence. By a providential fate the Greek artist had so faithfully portrayed the Wise Men as Persian Zoroastrians in the mosaic tableaux above the capitals that when the Persian hordes destroyed all the other churches in the country in 614 A.D., the Church of the Nativity was spared. "Are they not Fire Worshippers like ourselves?" said the leader as he withdrew his band from the church.

Raised up on yonder stone octagon, amid the splendor of chivalry, sat Godfrey de Buillon on his coronation throne. But when the vicar came to place the crown on his head, he pushed it aside, saying, "If my Lord received a crown of thorns, how can I accept a crown of gold?" Godfrey, the "Uncrowned King of Jerusalem."

But it is the lowly stable of an inn that we seek below these gaudy trappings and high altars. Descending by a half-circular stairway worn and shiny with candle wax, we come into a dark cave filled with incense and smoke which can only escape up the staircases. The ceilings and walls are clustered with hanging lamps whose tapers, floating in olive oil, give out a glimmer like that of glowworms restricting detail to an atmosphere unique in this crypt.

As the eye accustoms itself to the dimness, we see a Turkish soldier, his rifle butt on the marble floor and bayonet fixed, standing like another statue. His business is to ensure that not a single object is touched by any save the authorized priest to whose sect the particular item belongs. The *status quo* must be maintained. Nothing must be added to or taken from, since that would alter the balance of ownership within the sacred precincts.

Then we hear the clank of iron heels, and the relief guard comes down. Taking a taper, the two soldiers pass round the crypt, noting and counting piece by piece, lamp by lamp, trinket by trinket, down to the very hooks for the lamp chains. From the manger they inch along to the silver star. Falling on his knees, but not to worship, the outgoing guard lays his musket on the floor, the bayonet and star touching points, and with his finger passes round its edges to count each separate stud which fastens the star to the marble floor. And so when the tally is completed, the new guard takes over.

One day, to his consternation, the guard found a stud missing from the star. In that dingy, confined spot he must have slept on his feet while someone, perhaps a tourist, may have pried off the piece of metal for a souvenir. The guard reported to the corporal, the corporal to his captain and up the line to the local governor. He in turn reported immediately to the pasha in Jerusalem, and, within a few hours, the grand vizir was studying this perplexing international incident in order to advise the sultan in Constantinople.

Soon the flare-up came, each sect trying to outdo the other in its zeal. In Bethlehem representative churchmen went with angry protests to the governor. In Jerusalem the several patriarchs with consular representatives protested to the pasha, while in Constantinople the ambassadors of Czarist Russia and France, representing, respectively, the Greek Orthodox and Roman Catholic churches in the Orient, conveyed to the grand vizir the indignation of their governments for this dereliction of duty to preserve the *status quo*. Ownership of the particular nail might have been lost track of, but whoever was allowed to replace it could forever claim possession. No sect would grant that privilege to any other, hence the dilemma. "For want of a nail" another war might be lost. Had not the Crimean War started over Czarist Russia's claim to the self-styled rôle of "protector of the Orthodox Christians" following a petty quarrel about "a few Greek priests"? "A nail in Thy Holy Place" had assumed a new significance.

Marching daily to school through the stately Damascus Gate, we passed a gypsy encampment which settled there for some months each year. We loved to "see the burning sparks that flew" from the gypsy blacksmith's anvil as he sat on his haunches, arms between upraised knees, hammering at a plowshare or axe, while his wife pumped the two skin bellows like a woman impatient with her dough. The women of the camp often came round, begging for food and clothing. They were also adept at "lifting." But the old chief was well known to us, and the camp was a source of considerable attraction for tourists whom we often guided there. Among these visitors was the noted anti-sectarian evangelist Gipsy Smith, for whom we translated. While speaking some dialect of their international language among themselves, these gypsies had to use Arabic outside the camp. Gipsy Smith found many resemblances in language and customs to the gypsies of America, and our gypsy friends were delighted to see a gentleman proud to claim kinship with them.

Two classmates in our school line were children of the governor of Bethlehem—an Arab Moslem and very dear friend whose life of service and nobility of character served again in those formative years to shatter the illusion of labeled religion and pride of sectarianism. "How many pieces do you Christians cut your Lord up into?" he once asked an over-zealous missionary always wrangling with those of other sects.

One day the governor told us the sequel to the missing nail and the restoration of the *status quo*. Being the first Arab to be appointed to such an important post by the Turkish overlords, he was, of course, much per-turbed over the situation. Taking a silversmith with him privately to the crypt, he had a duplicate stud made, costing about fifty cents. But how and by whom could it be put into place? The silversmith, being a Christian, had to be eliminated. No Jew could be given this assignment, and neither could a Mohammedan. Finally the governor had an inspiration—our gypsy blacksmith! No one could accuse the gypsy of belonging to any sect or political faction. So, in the presence of the high and holy, diplomats and patriarchs, the lonely, isolated gypsy was the only one fully qualified to restore the sign of the Wise Men that radiated from this fountainhead of Christianity.

Each time, as I enter a church or chapel, I wonder—Is the creed that prevents its adherents from rising to the level of service that the lowliest of unbelievers can perform worthy of its name? And these lines from Masefield seem to give the reply:

> *I have seen flowers come in stony places.*
> *And kind deeds done by men with ugly faces,*
> *And the gold cup won by the worst horses in the races,*
> *So I trust too.*

Childhood Remembrance of Christmas

by Viola Jordanoff Bowman

I DO not know why, but even today Christmas, of all the Bulgarian holidays, arouses in me a peculiarly deep feeling. Is it because of the traditional customs that always take place during this season?

On Christmas Eve at home the little candles burn and everything is neat and peaceful and as quiet as if in church. My mother burns incense and spreads it all over the house, to the tiniest nook and corner. Is it because in the half-dark room the short flame of the tiny light twinkles in front of the images of the holiest mother and the little Christ? Is it because in the hearth burns the eve-wood, the largest piece of which we have kept for the holidays? Its flames run over the wall like fearful shadows. Or is it because our supper is quite unusual: all of us stand round the table quietly repeating after my father the Lord's Prayer . . . my father offers grateful words for the abundance of things displayed—the saltless, freshly made bread, the long red peppers stuffed with rice, the pickles and sauerkraut, the walnuts, the compote of dry fruits.

After this wonderful supper I can hardly wait my turn to kiss my father and mother's hands, to receive the long-awaited gift from my father who has already forgiven us for having been naughty and has smilingly asked us to follow his own example, the example of this Youth.

And what of Christmas morning, when, with the other children of the neighborhood, we go from house to house at the first chime of the church bell to sing Christmas carols?

The snow glitters in the sunshine and sounds crisp under our feet. The cold pinches our rosy cheeks. Our hands are half-frozen. In spite of these discomforts, at every door in the neighborhood our voices rise up in Christmas song. We know that we bring joy. Our hearts are warm with the thought that we follow Christ's road. And in this glorious joy we continue with the others to the tiny church for prayer.

Although the picture is not very different from that of Christmas everywhere, it is simple, full of feeling and atmosphere. In a word, it is a gem.

Three Christmas Classics

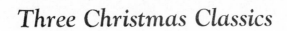

The Cratchits' Christmas

from "A Christmas Carol" by Charles Dickens

THEN up rose Mrs. Cratchit, Cratchit's wife, dressed out but poorly in a twice-turned gown, but brave in ribbons, which are cheap and make a goodly show for sixpence; and she laid the cloth, assisted by Belinda Cratchit, second of her daughters, also brave in ribbons; while Master Peter Cratchit plunged a fork into the saucepan of potatoes, and getting the corners of his monstrous shirt collar (Bob's private property, conferred upon his son and heir in honor of the day) into his mouth. And now two smaller Cratchits, boy and girl, came tearing in, screaming that outside the baker's they had smelled the goose, and known it for their own; and basking in luxurious thoughts of sage and onion, these young Cratchits danced about the table, and exalted Master Peter Cratchit to the skies, while he (not proud, although his collar nearly choked him) blew the fire, until the slow potatoes bubbling up, clamored loudly to be let out and peeled.

"What has ever got your precious father, then?" said Mrs. Cratchit. "And your brother, Tiny Tim! And Martha warn't as late last Christmas Day by half-an-hour!"

"Here's Martha, mother," said a girl, appearing as she spoke.

"Here's Martha, mother!" cried the two young Cratchits. "Hurrah! There's such a goose, Martha!"

"Why, bless your heart alive, my dear, how late you are!" said Mrs. Cratchit, kissing her a dozen times, and taking off her shawl and bonnet for her with officious zeal.

"We'd a deal of work to finish up last night," replied the girl, "and had to clear away this morning, mother!"

"Well! Never mind, so long as you are come," said Mrs. Cratchit. "Sit ye down before the fire, my dear, and have a warm, Lord bless ye!"

"No, no! There's father coming," cried the two young Cratchits, who were everywhere at once. "Hide, Martha, hide!"

So Martha hid herself, and in came little Bob, the father, with at least three foot of comforter exclusive of the fringe hanging down before him; and his threadbare clothes darned up and brushed, to look seasonable; and Tiny Tim upon his shoulder. Alas for Tiny Tim, he bore a little crutch, and had his limbs supported by an iron frame!

"Why, where's our Martha?" cried Bob Cratchit, looking around.

"Not coming," said Mrs. Cratchit.

"Not coming!" said Bob, with a sudden declension in his high spirits; for he had been Tim's blood horse all the way from church, and had come home rampant. "Not coming upon Christmas Day!"

Martha didn't like to see him disappointed, if it were only in joke, so she came out prematurely from behind the closet door, and ran into his arms, while the two young Cratchits hustled Tiny Tim, and bore him off into the wash-house, that he might hear the pudding singing in the copper.

"And how did little Tim behave?" asked Mrs. Cratchit, when she had rallied Bob on his credulity, and Bob had hugged his daughter to his heart's content.

"As good as gold," said Bob, "and better. Somehow, he gets thoughtful, sitting by himself so much, and thinks the strangest things you ever heard. He told me, coming home, that he hoped the people saw him in the church, because he was a cripple, and it might be pleasant to them to remember upon Christmas Day who made lame beggars walk and blind men see."

There never was such a goose. Bob said he didn't believe there ever was such a goose cooked. Its tenderness and flavor, size and cheapness, were the themes of universal admiration. Eked out by applesauce and mashed potatoes, it was a sufficient dinner for the whole family; indeed, as Mrs. Cratchit said with great delight (surveying one small atom of a bone upon the dish), they hadn't ate it all at last! Yet every one had had enough, and the youngest Cratchits, in particular, were steeped in sage and onion to the eyebrows! But now, the plates were being changed by Miss Belinda, Mrs. Cratchit left the room alone—too nervous to bear witness —to take the pudding and bring it in.

Suppose it should not be done enough! Suppose it should break in turning out! Suppose somebody should have got over the wall of the back yard and stolen it, while they were merry with the goose—a supposition at which the two young Cratchits became livid! All sorts of horrors were supposed.

Hallo! A great deal of steam! The pudding was out of the copper. A smell like a washing day! That was the cloth. A smell like an eating-house and a pastry cook's next door to each other, with a laundress' next to that! That was the pudding! In half a minute Mrs. Cratchit entered— flushed, but smiling proudly—with the pudding, like a speckled cannon ball, so hard and firm, blazing in half of half-a-quartern of ignited brandy, and bedight with Christmas holly stuck into the top.

Oh, a wonderful pudding! Bob Cratchit said, and calmly, too, that he regarded it as the greatest success achieved by Mrs. Cratchit since their marriage. Mrs. Cratchit said that now the weight was off her mind, she would confess she had her doubts about the quantity of flour. Everybody had something to say about it, but nobody said or thought it was at all a small pudding for a large family. It would have been flat heresy to do so. Any Cratchit would have blushed to hint at such a thing.

At last the dinner was all done, the cloth was cleared, the hearth swept and the fire made up. The compound in the jug being tasted and considered perfect, apples and oranges were put upon the table, and a shovel full of chestnuts on the fire. Then all the Cratchit family drew round the hearth, in which Bob Cratchit called a circle, meaning half a one; and at Bob Cratchit's elbow stood the family display of glass—two tumblers and a custard cup without a handle.

These held the hot stuff from the jug, however, as well as golden goblets would have done; and Bob served it out with beaming looks, while the chestnuts on the fire sputtered and cracked noisily.

Then Bob proposed: "A Merry Christmas to us all, my dears. God bless us!"

Which all the family re-echoed.

"God bless us every one!" said Tiny Tim, the last of all.

The Fir Tree

by Hans Christian Andersen

ONCE upon a time there was a pretty, green little Fir Tree. The sun shone on him; he had plenty of fresh air; and around him grew many large comrades, pines as well as firs. But the little Fir was not satisfied. He did not think of the large sun and the fresh air. He wanted to be a big tree like the others.

Sometimes the little children living in the cottages nearby came into the woods to play. "What a nice little Fir!" they said. But the Tree did not like to hear them talk this way. He did not like to be called "little."

By the time he was a year old he had grown a good deal. Another year passed and he was another long bit taller. "Oh, if I were only as tall as the other trees," he thought. "Then I could spread out my branches and look out into the wide world. The birds would build nests in my branches; and when there was a breeze I could bend with a stately bow just like the others."

The Tree sighed, taking no pleasure in the sunbeams and the birds and the red clouds, which morning and evening sailed above him.

In the winter time, when the snow lay white and glittering on the ground, a hare would often come leaping along. Sometimes he jumped right over the little Tree, and that made him very angry. But by the third winter the Tree had grown so large the hare had to go around it. That made the Tree feel better. "The most delightful thing in the world," he thought, "is to grow and grow and be tall and old."

In autumn the woodcutters came and cut down some of the largest trees. This happened every year and the little Fir Tree, which was not so little any more, was frightened. How he trembled as the magnificent trees fell to the earth with a great noise. After the branches had been lopped off, the trees looked so long and bare that it was hard to recognize them. Then they were laid in carts, and the horses dragged them out of the woods.

"What becomes of them?" the Fir Tree wondered.

In spring, when the Swallows and the Storks came, the Tree said to them, "Do you know where they have been taken?"

The Swallows did not know anything about it, but one of the Storks nodded his head thoughtfully. "I think I know," he said. "As I was flying hither from Egypt, I met many ships with tall masts and they smelt of fir. You may feel proud of them, so majestic did they look."

"If I were only old enough to fly across the ocean!" sighed the Tree. "How does the ocean look?"

"That would take a long time to explain," said the Stork, and off he flew.

"Rejoice in thy youth!" said the Sunbeams. "Rejoice in thy growth!" And the Wind kissed the tree; the Dew wept tears over him; but the Fir did not understand.

When Christmas came, many young trees were cut down. Their branches were left on them when they were laid on the carts, and the horses drew them out of the woods.

"They are no taller than I," complained the Fir Tree. "Indeed one of them was much shorter. Why are they allowed to keep all their branches? Where are they going?"

"We know! We know!" twittered the Sparrows. "We have peeped in at the windows in the town below! We saw the trees planted in the middle of the warm rooms and ornamented with the most splendid things — with gilded apples, with gingerbread, with toys and hundreds of lights!"

A tremor ran through the Fir Tree. "And then? What happens after that?"

"We did not see anything more, but it was very beautiful."

"Ah, perhaps I shall know the same magnificence some day," the Tree rejoiced. "If Christmas would only come! I am as tall as the trees that were carried off last year. Oh, if I were only on the cart now! If I were only in the warm room with all the splendor! Something better, something still grander, is sure to follow — but what? How I long, how I suffer! I wonder what is the matter with me!"

"Rejoice in us!" said the Air and the Sunlight. "Rejoice in thy own youth!"

But the Tree did not rejoice. He grew and grew. He was green both winter and summer. "What a fine tree!" people said, and toward Christmas he was one of the first to be cut down. The axe struck deep, and the Tree fell to earth with a sigh. He was not happy; he could only think how sad it was to be taken away from the place where he had sprung up. He knew that never again would he see his dear old comrades, the little bushes and flowers around him; perhaps he would never even see the birds again. And he didn't like it at all.

The Tree was laid on a cart with several others and taken away. When he came to himself again, he was being unloaded in a big yard, and two servants in handsome livery carried him into a beautiful drawing room. The Fir Tree was stuck upright in a tub filled with sand; but it did not look like a tub, for green cloth was hung all around it and it stood on a large, bright carpet.

A tremor ran through the Tree. What was going to happen? Several young ladies decorated it, aided by the servants. On one branch they hung little nets made of colored paper and filled with sugar-plums. On the other boughs they hung gilded apples and walnuts which looked as though they had grown there. Then little blue and white and red candles were fastened to the branches. Among the foliage there were dolls which looked like people — the Tree had never seen anything like them before — and at the very top there was a large star of gold tinsel. It was really splendid — too splendid for any words to describe.

"Just wait till evening!" everybody said. "How the Tree will shine this evening!"

"Oh, if evening would only come!" thought the Tree. "If the candles were only lighted! What will happen then, I wonder. Will the other trees from the forest come to look at me? Will the sparrows beat against the windowpanes? Perhaps I shall take root and stand here winter and summer covered with ornaments!" He grew so impatient that he got a pain in his bark, and this with trees is the same as a headache with us.

When at last the candles were lighted, there was such brightness, such splendor; the Tree trembled in every bough. One of the candles set fire to the foliage, and it blazed up splendidly.

"Help! Help!" cried the young ladies and rushed to put out the fire.

After that the Tree did not dare tremble. He was quite bewildered by the glare and the brightness. Suddenly both the folding doors opened, and in rushed the children, with the older persons following more quietly. The little ones stood quite still, but only for a moment. Then they shouted for joy, and the room echoed with their shouts. They began dancing around the Tree, pulling off one present after another.

"What are they doing?" thought the Tree. "What is to happen now?"

The candles burned down to the very branches, and as they burned down they were put out, one after another. Then the children were given permission to plunder the Tree, and they rushed upon it so violently that all its branches cracked. Then the children went on playing with their beautiful toys. No one even looked at the Tree, except the old nurse, who peeped in among the branches to see if there was a fig or an apple that had been overlooked.

"A story! A story!" the children cried, dragging a little fat man over toward the Tree. He sat down under it and said, "Now the Tree can listen, too. I shall tell you only one story, so which will you have: the one about Ivedy-Avedy, or the one about Klumpy-Dumpy who fell downstairs and yet married the princess and came to the throne after all?"

"Ivedy-Avedy!" cried some. "Klumpy-Dumpy!" cried others. There was a great deal of squealing, and finally the man told about Klumpy-Dumpy and the children clapped their hands and cried, "Go on! Go on!" The Fir Tree stood quite still, thinking, "Who knows? Perhaps I shall fall downstairs, too, and marry a princess!" And he looked forward to the next day, when he hoped to be decked out again with lights and toys and bright tinsel.

"I won't tremble tomorrow," he thought. "Tomorrow I shall hear again the story of Klumpy-Dumpy and perhaps that of Ivedy-Avedy, too." And all night long the Tree stood quite still, thinking.

The next morning in came the servants.

"Ah, now the splendor will begin again!" thought the Fir.

But no. The servants dragged him out of the room, up the stairs into the attic and there, in a dark corner, they left him. "What can this mean?" wondered the Tree, and he leaned against the wall lost in thought. And he had plenty of time for thinking. Days and nights passed and nobody came near him. When at last somebody did come up to the attic, it was only to leave some trunks. There stood the Tree quite hidden. There stood the Tree quite forgotten.

"It is winter out-of-doors!" he thought. "The earth is hard and covered with snow. I could not be planted now. These people are really very kind. They have put me up here under shelter until spring comes! If only it were not so dark and lonely here! Not even a hare! I liked it out in the woods when the snow was on the ground and the hare leaped by; yes, even when he jumped over me. Ah, but I did not like it then."

"Squeak, squeak!" said a little Mouse, peeping out of his hole. Then another little Mouse came and they sniffed at the Fir Tree and ran in and out among the branches.

"It is dreadfully cold," said the Mouse. "Except for that, it would be nice here, wouldn't it, old Fir?"

"I am not old," said the Fir Tree. "There is many a tree much older than I."

"Where do you come from?" asked the Mice. "Tell us about the most beautiful place in the world. Have you ever been there? Have you ever been in the larder where there are cheeses lying on the shelves and hams hanging from the ceiling, where one may dance on tallow candles; a place where one goes in lean and comes out fat?"

"I know of no such place," said the Tree. "But I know the woods where the sun shines and the birds sing." Then he told of the time when he was young, and the little Mice had never heard the like before.

"How much you have seen!" they said. "How happy you must have been!"

"I?" said the Fir Tree, thinking it over. "Yes, those really were happy times." Then he told about Christmas Eve, when he had been decked out with beautiful ornaments.

"Oh," said the little Mice. "How lucky you have been, old Fir Tree."

"I am not old," said he. "I came from the woods only this winter."

"But what wonderful stories you know!" said the Mice, and the next night they came with four other little Mice who wanted to hear the stories also. The more the Fir Tree talked about his youth, the more plainly he remembered it himself, and he realized that those times had really been very happy times. "But they may come again. Klumpy-Dumpy fell downstairs and yet he married a princess," said the Fir Tree.

"Who is Klumpy-Dumpy?" asked the Mice. So the Fir Tree told the story, and the little Mice were so pleased they jumped to the very top of the Tree. The next night two more Mice came and heard the story too.

At last the little Mice stopped coming, and the Tree sighed. "After all, I liked having the sleek little Mice listen to my stories, but that is over now. When I am brought out again I am going to enjoy myself."

But when was that to be? Why, one morning a number of people came up to the attic. Trunks were moved and the Tree was pulled out and thrown down on the floor. Then a man drew him toward the stairs, where the sun shone.

"Now life begins again," thought the Tree. He felt the fresh air, the first sunbeam — and then he was out in the yard. Roses hung over the fence and lindens were in bloom.

"Now I shall enjoy life," said the Tree, and spread out his branches. But alas, they were all withered and yellow. He lay in a corner among weeds and nettles. The golden star was still on the Tree, and it glittered in the sunlight.

In the yard some children were playing — the same children who had danced around the Fir Tree at Christmas time. They were glad to see him again, and the youngest child ran up and tore off the golden star.

"Look what is still on the ugly old Christmas Tree!" said he. And he trampled on the crackling branches.

The Tree looked at the beautiful garden and then at himself. He wished he had stayed in his dark corner in the loft. He thought of his youth in the woods, of the merry Christmas Eve, and of the little Mice.

" 'Tis over," said the poor Tree. "Had I but been happy when I had reason to be! But 'tis over now."

Then the gardener's boy chopped the Tree into small pieces for firewood. When it flamed up in the fireplace, it sighed deeply, and each sigh was like a shot.

The children went on playing in the yard. On his chest the youngest wore the gold star which the Tree had had on the happiest evening of his life. But that was over now — the Tree gone, the story finished.

A Visit From St. Nicholas

by Clement C. Moore

'TWAS the night before Christmas, and all through the house
Not a creature was stirring, not even a mouse;
The stockings were hung by the chimney with care,
In hopes that St. Nicholas soon would be there.
The children were nestled all snug in their beds,
While visions of sugar plums danced in their heads;
And Mamma in her kerchief, and I in my cap,
Had just settled down for a long winter's nap;
When out on the lawn there arose such a clatter,
I sprang from the bed to see what was the matter.
Away to the window I flew like a flash,
Tore open the shutters and threw up the sash.
The moon on the breast of the new-fallen snow
Gave the luster of midday to objects below;
When, what to my wondering eyes should appear,
But a miniature sleigh, and eight tiny reindeer,
With a little old driver so lively and quick,
I knew in a moment it must be St. Nick.
More rapid than eagles his coursers they came,
And he whistled and shouted and called them by name,
"Now, Dasher! now, Dancer! now, Prancer! now, Vixen!
On Comet! on Cupid, on Dunder and Blixen!
To the top of the porch, to the top of the wall,
Now dash away, dash away, dash away all!"
As dry leaves that before the wild hurricane fly,
When they meet with an obstacle, mount to the sky,
So up to the housetop the coursers they flew,

With the sleigh full of toys and St. Nicholas, too;
And then, in a twinkling, I heard on the roof
The prancing and pawing of each tiny hoof.
As I drew in my head and was turning around,
Down the chimney St. Nicholas came with a bound.
He was dressed all in fur from his head to his foot,
And his clothes were all tarnished with ashes and soot;
A bundle of toys he had flung on his back
And he looked like a peddler just opening his pack.
His eyes, how they twinkled! his dimples, how merry!
His cheeks were like roses, his nose like a cherry,
His droll little mouth was drawn up like a bow,
And the beard on his chin was as white as the snow.
The stump of a pipe he held tight in his teeth,
And the smoke it encircled his head like a wreath.
He had a broad face, and a round little belly,
That shook, when he laughed, like a bowl full of jelly.
He was chubby and plump, a right jolly old elf,
And I laughed when I saw him, in spite of myself.
A wink of his eye and a twist of his head
Soon gave me to know I had nothing to dread.
He spoke not a word, but went straight to his work,
And filled all the stockings — then turned with a jerk
And laying his finger aside of his nose,
And giving a nod, up the chimney he rose.
He sprang to his sleigh, to his team gave a whistle,
And away they all flew like the down of a thistle;
But I heard him exclaim, ere he drove out of sight,
"Merry Christmas to all, and to all a good night!"

Four Christmas Poems

A Prince of Peace

ONCE each dying year,
Joyful to appear,
Comes from heav'n afar
Nativity's star.

Above the town,
Woodland and down,
It shines to earth
On Nature's birth.

The great of the land
In humbleness stand,
Children once more
Whom a mother bore.

In castle or stable,
In manger or cradle,
Bedded in hay,
A Jesus could lay.

Cattle may low
Or trumpets blow,
Kings' ransoms pour
And shepherds adore;

But Wise Men ponder—
"In swaddling yonder,
Life may release
A Prince of Peace."

—LARS ERIKSSON LIND

Christmas

CHRISTMAS is warmth in the heart
    and cold outside;
        cold, crisp stars over
            glistening snow.

Christmas is a package
    wrapped in love,
        Christ love.

Christmas is a world together
    smaller, easier
        animated by goodness.

From me to you Christmas
    stars in the heart
        love in the world
            serenity.

—FLORENCE ROME GARRETT

A Winter Day

'TIS Christmas again and once more as before
We hang up the holly outside the front door.
The hills and valleys are covered with snow,
Brushed with crystals of ice that glow
From towering trees, from shrubs, each tiny strand
Glistens in winter's fairyland.
The snow, like a veil, drawn across earth's face,
Falls from each branch like frothy lace
And the wind fingers lightly hill and plain,
Chanting a soft cathedral strain;
Through the windowed trees, the sun's clear, bright gaze
Cloaks the world in a golden haze,
Transforming this earthly vision of ice
To reflection of Paradise.
'Tis Christmas again and once more as before
We hang up the holly outside the front door.

—MARGARET PHILLIPS SUCCOP

GOD bless the little things
this Christmastide;
All the little wild things
that live outside,
Little cold robins and
rabbits in the snow,
Give them good faring
and a warm place to go.
All the little young things
for His sake who died,
Who was a little thing
at Christmastide.

—AUTHOR UNKNOWN

Christmas Carols and Decorations

Christmas Carols — Their History

by Marion R. Todd

THE word "carol," coming from the old French *carole*, means a kind of dance. In medieval Europe the early carols were danced by groups as they sang with gaiety. The middle English carol was a round dance to joyous song or lyric. The church accepted these carols in its services as songs of joy or praise in honor of the Nativity, even though they were pagan in spirit, some dating back to the Roman Saturnalia (*choraules*, choral dance to a flute) and the Druid ceremonies.

Early in the thirteenth century in Italy, St. Francis set up in his church a little cradle called a crèche or praesepium. Here the custom of the Magi drama was immortalized with gifts brought by the children of

his parish, and here too the many beautiful carols and lullaby songs originated.

Scholars believe the hymn "Adeste Fideles" (Come All Ye Faithful) was also part of the early Christmas celebration and was danced before the crèche.

The Anglo-Saxons drank a toast to the Lord at Christmastide— "Wassail," or in old Norse, *Ves heill*, meaning "Be in health."

Today many countries celebrate religious dances in their churches at Christmastime. Choirboys enter the Cathedral of Seville in a sacred dance with castanets to pay their homage. This ritual also occurs throughout the Americas where the early Spanish missionaries first ventured.

It is said that "carols are the layman's most beautiful contribution to his religion."

"O Little Town of Bethlehem" is one of our few American Christmas carols. This popular carol was written by Phillip Brooks. The organist of Dr. Brooks's church, Lewis Redner, composed the music in 1868.

In 1840 Felix Mendelssohn-Bartholdy wrote a cantata to commemorate the invention of printing. Charles Wesley, brother of the famous John Wesley, wrote the lyrics of "Hark the Herald Angels Sing," using the second chorus of Mendelssohn's famous work.

In 1818 in the little Bavarian town of Oberndorf, Franz Gruber, a schoolmaster, and Josef Mohr, assistant village priest, wrote the lovely *Stille Nacht* ("Silent Night"), perhaps the most familiar and beloved carol in the world.

"The First Noel" is one of the oldest of medieval Christmas carols sung by shepherds in France and England.

O Little Town of Bethlehem

NOT TOO FAST

O lit - tle town of Beth - le - hem, How still we see thee lie!
For Christ is born of Ma - ry, And gath - ered all a - bove,
O ho - ly Child of Beth - le - hem! De - scend to us, we pray;

A - bove thy deep and dream - less sleep The si - lent stars go by;
While mor - tals sleep, the an - gels keep Their watch of won - dering love.
Cast out our sin, and en - ter in, Be born in us to day!

Yet in thy dark street shin - eth The ev - er - last - ing Light;
O morn - ing stars, to - geth - er Pro - claim the ho - ly birth,
We hear the Christ - mas an - gels The great glad tid - ings tell;

The hopes and fears of all the years Are met in thee to - night.
And prais - es sing to God our King, And peace to men on earth!
O come to us, a - bide with us, Our Lord Im - man - u - el!

Hark the Herald Angels Sing

MAESTOSO

1. Hark! the her - ald an - gels sing, "Glo - ry to the new-born King;
2. Hail the heav'n-born Prince of Peace! Hail the Sun of right-eous-ness!

Peace on earth, and mer - cy mild; God and sin - ners rec - on - ciled."
Light and life to all He brings, Risen with heal - ing in His Wings.

Joy - ful, all ye na - tions rise, Join the tri - umph of the skies;
Mild He lays His glo - ry by, Born that man no more may die,

With an - gel - ic hosts pro - claim, "Christ is born in Beth - le - hem!"
Born to raise the sons of earth, Born to give them sec - ond birth.

Hark! the her - ald an - gels sing, "Glo - ry to the new-born King."

Silent Night

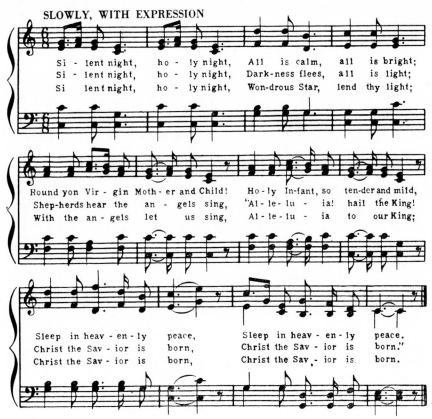

SLOWLY, WITH EXPRESSION

Si - lent night, ho - ly night, All is calm, all is bright;
Si - lent night, ho - ly night, Dark-ness flees, all is light;
Si - lent night, ho - ly night, Won-drous Star, lend thy light;

Round yon Vir - gin Moth - er and Child! Ho - ly In-fant, so ten-der and mild,
Shep-herds hear the an - gels sing, "Al - le - lu - ia! hail the King!
With the an - gels let us sing, Al - le - lu - ia to our King;

Sleep in heav - en - ly peace, Sleep in heav - en - ly peace.
Christ the Sav - ior is born, Christ the Sav - ior is born."
Christ the Sav - ior is born, Christ the Sav - ior is born.

Jingle Bells

ALLEGRO

1. — Dash-ing thro' the snow In a one horse o-pen sleigh, —
2. A day or two a-go I thought I'd take a ride, And

o'er the fields we go, — Laugh-ing all the way; —
soon Miss Fan-nie Bright Was seat-ed by my side; The

Bells on bob-tail ring, — Mak-ing spir-its bright, What
horse was lean and lank, Mis-for-tune seem'd his lot, He

fun it is to ride and sing A sleigh-ing song to-night!
got in-to a drift-ed bank, And we, we got up-sot.

CHORUS

Jin-gle bells! jin-gle bells! Jin-gle all the way! Oh, what fun it is to ride in a

1. one-horse o-pen sleigh!

2. one-horse o-pen sleigh!

The First Noel

MODERATELY

1. The first No-el, the an-gels did say, Was to cer-tain poor
2. They look-ed up and saw a star shin-ing in the
3. Then en-tered in the wise-men three, Full rev-er-ent-

shep-herds in fields as they lay; In fields where they lay
east, be-yond them far, And to the earth it
ly up-on their knee, And of-fered there, in

keep-ing their sheep, On a cold win-ter's night that was so deep.
gave great light, And so it con-tin-ued both day and night.
His pres-ence, Their gold and myrrh and frank-in-cense.

REFRAIN.

No-el, No-el, No-el, No-el, Born is the King of Is-ra-el.

The Origin and Meaning
of Christmas Decorations

by Marion R. Todd

F ROM various lands comes the custom of decorating our homes at Christmastime.

Bringing the Christmas tree into the home is attributed to Martin Luther in the early half of the sixteenth century. However, an earlier version of the Christmas tree saga goes back to the eighth century, when St. Winifred, a missionary from Britain to Germany, came upon a group sacrificing a young boy to Thor, the god of thunder. He explained to these people that Jesus did not ask for human sacrifice, but for service to others. Pointing to a little fir tree standing alone by a large fallen oak, St. Winifred said; "Let us call it the tree of the Christ child."

In early times the Romans celebrated a feast to Saturn, their god of agriculture, at about the same time of the year we celebrate our Christmas. They used the holly evergreen to decorate their homes for this festival. In many European countries holly would not be used at Christmas because of its pagan origin. In England, however, holly was popular at an early date; in fact, in the eighteenth century holly and ivy were the symbols of fertility. Holly is also known as the Christ-thorn, since its red berries and prickly leaves remind us of the drops of blood on the crown of thorns worn by Jesus.

In 70 A.D. Joseph of Arimathea traveled to Britain, where he built a church of twigs. He placed his staff in the ground, whence grew a lovely small tree called the hawthorn, which blossoms at Christmas with fragant flowers of white, pink or red, and red berries.

Earliest records of the rosemary plant note its existence during the flight into Egypt to escape King Herod's wrath. Mary is supposed to have placed the Christ child's garments on this evergreen shrub. The original flowers were white, but because the Virgin Mary wore pale purple, the plant changed its color to match her robes.

Also associated with this famous flight is the rose of Jericho, which, according to legend, grew wherever Mary stopped. Its oval leaves and spikes of small white flowers curl up when dry and expand when moistened.

The bay tree with its purple berries and lacy leaves is supposed to have protected Mary, Joseph and the Christ child during the many

thunderstorms. In olden times people would decorate their homes with its lovely branches at Christmas for protection during the coming year against storms and lightning.

One of our most beautiful Christmas plants is the poinsettia. It was brought from Mexico to South Carolina in 1829 by Dr. Joel Roberts Poinsett, the American ambassador to Mexico, after whom the plant is named. There is the lovely legend that one evening a little Mexican girl was on her way to church; having no gift for the baby Jesus, she knelt and prayed. Arising, a most beautiful flower appeared before her—a shrub with yellow flowers surrounded by tapering red leaves resembling petals, it is often called the "flower of the Holy Night."

One of our Christmas decorations which causes much gaiety is the mistletoe. This yellowish-green plant, used by the ancient Druids in England and France in their religious ceremonies, is now by custom an excuse to kiss the one you admire standing under it!

In this Christmas season let us indeed "deck the halls with boughs of holly!"

The Christmas Hope

THAT night when in the Judean skies
The mystic star dispensed its light,
A blind man moved in his sleep—
And dreamed that he had sight!

That night when shepherds heard the song
Of hosts angelic choiring near,

A deaf man stirred in slumber's spell—
And dreamed that he could hear!

That night when in the cattle stall
Slept child and mother, cheek by jowl,
A cripple turned his twisted limbs—
And dreamed that he was whole!

That night when o'er the new-born babe
The tender Mary rose to lean,
A loathsome leper smiled in sleep—
And dreamed that he was clean!

That night when to the mother's breast
The little King was pressed secure,
A harlot slept a happy sleep—
And dreamed that she was pure!

That night when in the manger lay
The sanctified who came to save,
A man moved in the sleep of death—
And dreamed there was no grave!

—AUTHOR UNKNOWN

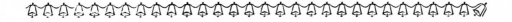

Among Our Contributors...

VIOLA JORDANOFF BOWMAN was born in Bulgaria and is a graduate of the Music Academy there. She was a featured singer over Bulgarian radio and in opera. During 1950-53 she broadcast for Radio Free Europe. She is married to Roger Bowman of the National Broadcasting Co. The Bowmans have one child and live in Old Greenwich, Connecticut.

COUNT FRANCIS G. DE SZECHENYI has taught in this country and in other parts of the world, and is chairman of the Foreign Languages Department at Alliance College in Cambridge Springs, Pennsylvania.

GERDA DE TOPKE, the wife of the Bolivian ambassador to Guatemala, has lived for many years in Guatemala, where she and her husband maintain large coffee plantations. She has traveled extensively throughout South America in the diplomatic corps.

FLORENCE ROME GARRETT lives in Connecticut and is a member of the National League of American Pen Women.

HEATHER HARRISON is the mother of six children and the wife of the director of foreign operations of International Technicolor, Inc. She has lived in Europe and in the Orient, and is a member of the National League of American Pen Women.

ROBERT HILLYER, Pulitzer Prize winner, whose position as the foremost lyric poet of his age appears secure, lives today in Newark, Delaware.

JACQUELINE (JACKIE) ANN HOOD, co-artist of this book, studied portrait, fashion, and water color art, is the mother of four boys, and claims skiing, bowling, and ceramics as her hobbies. Her husband, Cal Hood, is the noted Connecticut photographer.

LADY MAY LAWFORD, the mother of screen, stage and television actor Peter Lawford, is a world traveler with that rare facility for capturing in prose the mores and customs of other lands. She resides, currently, in Los Angeles.

LARS ERIKSSON LIND, Swedish-born, says that his parents were drawn irresistibly to Palestine in 1896. Having been himself an eyewitness to the trials which have beset this perennially troubled region, he writes out of a deep sense of sympathy for the country and its inhabitants. Mr. Lind currently makes his home in California.

PHYLLIS LUNDELL, co-artist of this volume, is a graduate of Pratt Institute and has exhibited at the Carnegie Institute in Pittsburgh. The mother of three young boys, she lives in Port Chester, New York.

PATRICK MAHONY, who has written extensively about Ireland and the Irish (*Out of the Silence* and *You Can Find a Way*), was, paradoxically, born in England and educated in the United States. Mr. Mahony, of whom the late Maurice Maeterlinck said: "he has tried to see as closely as possible into the hearts of the Irish people..." is a former staff member of King Features Syndicate.

GLADYS AND RAY OWEN, honorary princess and chief, respectively, of the Blackfeet Nation, are perhaps best known for the wealth of Indian lore which they have presented on film to lecture audiences throughout the country. Mr. Owen is a descendant of Kit Carson and was graduated from Yale. He is a member of the Explorers Club. Mrs. Owen is a member of the National League of American Pen Women and the Society of Woman Geographers. They are members of the Royal Society of Literature of Great Britain.

Evelyn Peterson is a Vassar graduate and has studied voice at the Julliard School of Music, the Berkshire Music Center and the University of Illinois. Her interest in the Christmas celebrations of the various countries developed during a series of concerts in which she appeared in the costumes native to the particular regions of which she sang. She is a member of the National League of American Pen Women.

Rosa L. Sheldon has lived in many countries and now resides in Mexico City.

Suzanne Silvercruys Stevenson, the daughter of the late Baron Silvercruys, president of the Belgian Supreme Court, came to the United States as a child who had witnessed German atrocities in World War i, and whose vivid descriptions of them induced the Belgian government to commission her as a lecturer here. Sculptor, author and playwright, she has been a candidate for the United States Senate from Connecticut.

Marion R. Todd, the editor of this volume, is a descendant of the Governor William Bradford, of whom she writes, and of Angell Husted, a founder of her native Greenwich, Connecticut. Prominently associated with an imposing roster of organizations, she is the founder of the Children of the American Revolution and the Children of the American Colonists, and is the founder and first president of the Greenwich, Connecticut, branch of the National League of American Pen Women.

Oguz R. Turkkan was born in Istanbul and has taught at Columbia University and the City College of New York. A publisher whose fight for a democratic regime in Turkey led to his arrest, he endured months of solitary confinement before his eventual release by the Turkish Supreme Court. His memoirs, published in 1955, attained best-seller status; and he is the co-author of *One America* (Prentice-Hall, 1951).

Margaret Phillips Succop lived in Pittsburgh and has been a contributor to *Modern American Sonnets*. One of her poems, "I Reached for Words," received an award from the American and British Poetry Society. She is a member of the National League of American Pen Women.

Nora Waln will be remembered for *House of Exile* (Little, Brown, 1933). The daughter of a Quaker family of Philadelphia, she has spent many years in the Orient and writes today from her home in England. She is a member of the International P.E.N. and the National League of American Pen Women.

Josephine Garibaldi Ziluca is the granddaughter of the Liberator of Italy. The mother of two sons, she now lives in Greenwich, Connecticut.

Friderike Zweig is an outstanding figure in contemporary German literature, with novels, poetry, biographies and translations to her credit. She is the author of *Stefan Zweig*, which has appeared in translation in this country, and is at present at work on a new novel. She is a member of the International P.E.N. and the National League of American Pen Women.

THE CHRISTMAS BOOK

CELEBRATING CHRISTMAS IN ALL NATIONS
EDITED BY MARION R. TODD

PERHAPS the best thing to be said about any year is that it includes Christmas. And perhaps the best thing to be said about *this* Christmas is that it marks the emergence of as charming a compilation of the hows and whys of the world's Christmas celebrations ever encased between covers, a book for young and old alike, without which no Christmas observance is truly complete.

The contributors to this volume have observed Christmas in many lands, and have been struck by the multiplicity of traditions and customs with which the various peoples of the world surround their celebrations. The day as it is honored in the United States is, of course, well known. Less familiar are the curiosa prevailing in Germany and Austria, where Nikolo, appearing in bishop's garments, embarks as early as December 6 on his gift-distributing errand, accompanied by a huge and fearsome fellow (the *Krampus*) whose special duty it is to frighten naughty children. Christmas in England, in Ireland, in the Orient has its own distinct flavor and embellishments; in Belgium, for example, St. Nicholas discards his sleigh for a simple cart drawn by a donkey; and in Italy and Mexico, France and Guatemala, Jerusalem and the Scandinavian countries the fact and fancy, the faith and folklore of Christmas adhered to are as timeless in their historical significance as they are delightful and picturesque. Indeed, the traditions cherished by *every* country—the carols, the tree, the decorations, and the various means of depicting the scene of the Nativity—are traced to their unique origins in this glowing volume.

(Continued on back flap)